DESIGN AND DEVELOPMENT OF PROGRAMS AS TEACHING MATERIAL

MEP Information Guide 3

DESIGN AND DEVELOPMENT OF PROGRAMS AS TEACHING MATERIAL

Hugh Burkhardt and Rosemary Fraser
with Max Clowes, Jim Eggleston
and Colin Wells

INVESTIGATIONS ON TEACHING WITH MICROCOMPUTERS AS AN AID

Council for Educational Technology on behalf of the Microelectronics Education Programme

Published and distributed by the Council for Educational Technology,
3 Devonshire Street, London W1N 2BA
on behalf of the Microelectronics Education Programme,
Newcastle upon Tyne Polytechnic,
Cheviot House,
Coach Lane Campus,
Newcastle upon Tyne NE7 7XA

First published 1982

ISSN 0262-2181
ISBN 0 86184-076-3

 British Library Cataloguing in Publication Data

Design and development of programs as teaching
materials.—(Microelectronics Education Programme information guide,
ISSN 0262-2181; 3)
1. Electronic digital computers — Programming
I. Burkhardt, Hugh
II. Series
001.64   QA76.6

ISBN 0-86184-076-3

Printed in Great Britain by
H Cave & Co Ltd
Cumberland Street
Leicester LE1 4QQ

Contents

6

Preface

The development of teaching material which will be found useful by a wide range of teachers has proved an intractable problem in every subject. The cost of developing teaching units involving the microcomputer as a teaching aid, with which we are concerned, justifies putting substantial efforts into tackling this challenge. We regard the problems of development and dissemination as being closely linked. We describe systematic methods of developing material which aim to ensure that it *is* useful to a wide range of teachers and that they can easily learn to use it effectively. The essential elements are imaginative design aimed at helping the teacher to stimulate specific learning activities, and the provision of feedback on the classroom use of material in the development-dissemination process. We argue that this must be largely based on classroom observation and we provide systematic methods for the collection of such information and for revising the programs and associated documentation in the light of it. Throughout the book we emphasize the classroom situation where a single micro is in use as a teaching aid – but a broadly similar approach is appropriate to the development of other teaching material, with or without computers.

Acknowledgements
This book is based on two papers prepared for the Microelectronics Education Programme. The authors would like to acknowledge their debt to all their colleagues in the collaboration Investigations on Teaching and Microcomputers as an Aid at the College of St Mark and St John and at the Shell Centre for Mathematical Education at the University of Nottingham, and elsewhere – the methods presented here for the development of effective teaching material of a novel kind have themselves been developed and tested through the work of the ITMA collaboration.

Ten-minute prologue

Let us assume you have a draft program — many computer enthusiasts who happen to be teachers have ideas about some programs that could be used in class. If, to take the simplest case, you only want it for your own use, you will try it in the classroom with the possible results that (i) it is OK as it is, (ii) it is no good at all, or (iii) it seems worth spending time making it better. If it is in the third group, you may just want to develop further your own ideas for your own use; if so, you may as well stop here — but otherwise read on.

If you want your program to be useful to other teachers you have a wider set of problems to tackle. You have to ensure that it fits in with their teaching ideas and styles and you have to let them know what its possibilities are and how they can realize them in the classroom. If you take these challenges on you will probably find that you too learn of new possibilities from the other teachers and pupils involved in developing the unit. The rest of this paper takes a hard look at some ideas on these development processes; much of what it says is mundane and obvious, but there may be some value in gathering it together so that the 'designer' does not overlook something important.

How may you proceed? There are various approaches. We will outline one — it will inevitably appear prescriptive but it is written in the spirit of 'here's one possibility — take a look at it — then decide how *you* wish to proceed'. We refer parenthetically to later sections in which particular issues are discussed in detail.

1. First find your other teachers
You have decided to share your idea, and your program (you have not got around to much documentation) in the hope of fame and fear of ridicule, and you want a bunch of lively, interested teachers to help develop it. You may find them in your school, at subject association meetings, at educational computing meetings or at a local curriculum development centre. It is better if you like one another: an easy social atmosphere helps criticism. If you have already got the draft program, you would have done better to have talked to the others long ago when the ideas were developing — maybe you will next time (see Chapter 2).

2. Next sell your program to them
You cannot tell if your 'unit' works for other teachers unless a fair number try it. No restraint or balance is needed yet: their reaction is no indication of popular appeal — they are as atypical as you are. Talk them into trying it any way you can — as a condition for a free copy, in exchange for trying one of theirs, in return for taking one of their classes, etc.

3. Teach them how to drive it

You know how your program works — its main theme and variations, and the teacher and pupil activities that you think should go with it. You have not written any of it down, of course. One day you will have to face getting it all over to an invisible audience, with only 10 minutes' patience (sympathize with us at this moment) but today you have enough problems without that. Take them through it a few times. If the bugs which you handle so effortlessly — RESET, change disc, B, BASICS, PEEK (12345) — distract your friends, promise to fix them (and even fix them). Then get one of them to try giving you all a lesson. It is entertaining for everyone. Now you are nearly ready for the thundering herd.

4. You have a go first

Most of us like to try the unit ourselves before letting others have a go. If you are a classroom teacher, this will be easy. You have probably written the unit for 4F anyway and they will get it whether they like it or not — and they probably will like it, compared with the day-to-day routine. If you no longer have such captive audiences, you will have to borrow them; this too is usually not too hard. But get the class teacher to observe what happens (see Chapter 3).

5. By now you really must write some notes

6. Arrange to watch the action

Get other teachers to agree to let you 'observe'. You will be astonished how ready most of us are to be watched — we respond well to a show of interest. The worst of the practical problems begin here (see Chapter 3). You have to be free when they are able to fit the unit into the (always crowded) curriculum of an appropriate class. (This is one reason why progress is easier and commoner in primary schools.) It pays to plan ahead. Persistence is the only hope, and is no guarantee.

7. Avoid that blank feeling

You will really enjoy watching your 'child' perform — though with a certain irritation that she is not quite at her best and feeling that she could have had a bigger part that stretched her talents more. Unless you went in prepared though (see Chapters 3 and 4) you will emerge wondering what happened — with a few, often false, impressions but not much idea what to do about them (see Chapter 5). This is the hardest part of developing effective units — collecting that priceless information that is flowing before your eyes (see Chapter 3) and drawing the right inferences from it (see Chapter 5) about how to change the program and documentation. We spend a fair bit of this paper describing how you may do it efficiently. But if you are strictly the 10-minute type, we suggest you go in with (i) some ideas about what you hope will happen, *emphasizing pupil and teacher activities;* (ii) some questions that you wanted answered about the unit (perhaps from the CHECKLISTS), and (iii) some paper to note what does happen in detail and in general. Our later suggestions (see Chapters 3, 4 and 5) are just a systematic way of doing this.

8. Turning information into action

Now you have to draw inferences about changes in the unit to minimize the disasters you have witnessed and enhance the educational impact (see Chapter 5). Changes will be needed, not only in the program but also in the teaching activities around it; the documentation will need to share your development experience with the user. The clearer your questions and record (see Chapter 3), the more straightforward and effective this stage will be.

9. Slaughtering the innocents

Now the unit 'works' with your cronies. The time has come to loose it on the world at large — but it pays to start gently (see Chapter 4). First try it on a detached but sympathetic colleague or two — definitely not of the 'computer-nut' brigade. You can still explain it — thus dodging the second great hurdle, coming next. These trials are a shade more 'realistic' and will give you further ideas, particularly on the difficulties of understanding and introducing the program that are likely to arise.

10. Telling the world

Now you really have to write it up, not only so people *can* understand and use it without your being there, but preferably so that they *will* do so (see Chapter 6). It is easy enough if your program does just one thing, like a film, but getting a 'driving system' (see Chapter 2) that will enable teachers easily to control a flexible program and documenting the unit so that its teaching possibilities are clear is hard — and may even be impossible. This paper looks at the problems; but it takes more than 10 minutes.

11. Making your fortune

Effective publication is also a problem (see Chapter 6).

Introduction

We now take a somewhat more thorough look at the processes of development of teaching material, from the generation of ideas through to the publication of units, linking the theoretical discussions and practical suggestions for the designers — whether they be individual teachers working on units in their spare time or a professional curriculum development team. It is for each group or designer to consider this rather daunting list and to decide which aspects they are able to include in their development process.

The production of good teaching material that can be used effectively by many teachers with a wide range of styles is a difficult task, as is the communication of the possibilities of the material to teachers who wish to use it. A lot of interesting curriculum development in many subjects has not had any large-scale impact. The programming and documentation of units using the microcomputer as a teaching aid is a time-consuming business, often taking several man-months of effort to turn a teaching idea into a reasonably robust draft unit that more or less works.

It seems worth putting a significant effort into educational design and classroom development in order to ensure that a teaching unit is widely useful to teachers. Here we discuss the process of turning an initial idea into a draft program with associated notes, and the subsequent development process, with an emphasis on getting relevant feedback from classroom trials. We address ourselves to the designer of the material, whether he is working alone or as part of a team.

Some may find the picture we paint forbidding — certainly it sets out a more systematic approach to curriculum development than is commonly applied and the activities it envisages may seem much less attractive than producing new teaching ideas and turning them into reasonable working programs. We have felt the same way ourselves but, though the organization is a chore, we have found that watching what happens in the classroom is invariably fascinating and often delightful; it has taught us more than anything else about learning and teaching and the materials that are supportive. The time involved has not proved to be a large proportion of the total effort. Do what you can.

Examples are helpful — but only if they are familiar. We shall illustrate our discussions by referring to various units produced by the ITMA/Shell Centre teams in Plymouth and Nottingham. These include PIRATES, JANEPLUS, TRANSPOTS and STORYLINE. For those who have not yet met these units, brief but adequate descriptions are given in Appendix A. You may like to read them now.

To give more direct practical aid to designers, we have crystallized our discussion into a set of checklists to be used at various stages of the development process. We recognize that others will want to modify them, or even start afresh, but the response to the draft versions of this work indicate that others have found them useful. They form Appendix B.

Our analysis is inevitably partial and provisional. Some of it is still merely based on an intuitive belief as to what is likely to work, but a substantial amount is based directly on our experience of classroom observation, though still little of this could be described as research in reasonably controlled situations. Many people have contributed — apart from our colleagues in the ITMA collaboration, we are particularly grateful to all those teachers who have worked with us and whose classrooms are the laboratories in which ideas are tested and improved and discoveries made.

The conclusions will become clearer and firmer as experience accumulates, provided it is related to some systematic framework such we have produced here. We look forward to this.

1. Design and development – the process, the team and the unit

Nine stages of development

What is the sequence of events? The plan below gives one possible guide to the process.

Writing	*Development*
1. State aims, targets, intentions, etc.	Discuss with interested group, observe lessons if relevant – brainstorm ideas. Check idea against aims, targets, etc. Discuss intentions, use draft checklist.
2. Ideas accepted – write down intentions and behaviour (see Chapter 2 and Checklists 1, 2, 3 and 4).	Establish the group of interested developers – think ahead to classroom lessons. If possible watch teachers with their normal lessons and get to know the background.
3. Draft the program into code with some minimum notes on how to operate it and what you hope for in the classroom (Chapter 2 and Checklists 2 and 5).	Discuss the draft program with the group – discuss lessons that could be given. Try it out on as many people as possible. Make sure it is easy enough to control (see Chapter 2 and Checklist 4).
4. Revision of draft program ready for first classroom trial.	Take the program into the classroom yourself, with others to observe if possible (see Chapter 3).
5. Write a report on the progress so far.	Decide whether to continue or abort at this stage.
6. More revision if necessary. In particular begin to make clear notes on the control of the program and start to map out teaching notes (see Chapter 6 and Checklist 4). These will expand as you receive development experience.	Other teachers within the group try it out in the classroom – again where possible with observers or with yourself as observer (see Chapters 3 and 6, and Checklists 3 and 4). You should prepare well for this stage (see Chapter 4).

7. Rewriting in view of the evidence. Give special consideration again to your stated intentions, etc, revised in the light of experience (see Chapter 5 and Checklists 1 and 3).

Continue to watch as many lessons as possible in order to get enough information for the final documentation. Try to include users who have used the unit several times, in particular to check that the driving system remains effective and does not become irritating with repetition (see Chapter 4).

8. The program must now be polished up to include enough 'user support', etc (see Chapter 5). Also the documentation must give as clear an indication as possible to the user of the teaching possibilities (see Chapter 6 and Checklist 3).

More trials with a wider audience − check that the 'driving system' helps to educate users in the use of the teaching unit (see Chapter 6 and Checklist 4) − also trials on the unit's documentation. The unit must be able to survive alone (see Chapter 6).

9. Final production of material suitable for publishing (see Chapter 6 and Checklist 5).

Final material should now be circulated to teachers for final comments and editing (see Chapters 4 and 6).

The nine stages of gestation of the unit will take a variable length of time depending on whether it turns out to be an 'elephant' or a 'mouse'.

The above table gives a summary of the development processes; the diagram below represents this in another form showing the roles of the development team.

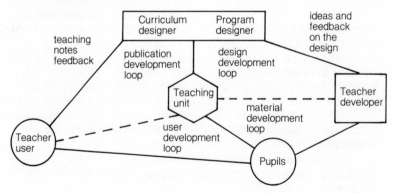

The development loops correspond very closely to the table of action but here we emphasize the four stages, which partly overlap; they depend on each other and may also involve a return to an earlier stage in the light of feedback.

Stage 1. Design development loop: involves the curriculum designer, program designer and teacher developers.

Stage 2. Material development loop: first trials in the classroom involving teacher developers and observers (often the curriculum designer and program designer) lead to the revision of the design and production of the first materials — both program and notes.

Stage 3. User development loop: moving out to wider trials and getting the most relevant feedback leading to more revision to ensure that the teaching unit can help to educate the unfamiliar user (this revision of the unit is aimed at helping the users to develop the ability to realize the unit's intentions). This stage involves the curriculum designer, program designer and teacher developers and teacher users, as well as observers.

Stage 4. Publication development loop: final decisions on the written unit as a result of all the trials, discussions and feedback from all involved, namely the whole team.

The design team
This process produced the unit — more about its possible form of publication is given in Chapter 6. The design team have a responsibility to help other teachers notice, look at, acquire, study and use the material with a minimum of effort. On page 35 we take a detailed look at ways of describing to the teacher how to 'drive the program' and how to use it in the classroom.

The design team may have many forms from a single individual working alone to a broadly based curriculum development team with specialists in curriculum design, graphics, programming and observation; however, for our purpose it is useful to emphasize three roles — the curriculum designer who has overall responsibility for the program teaching unit and its associated written or audio-visual material, the program designer who realizes the computer program and the teacher developers in whose classrooms the material is tried and tuned. In practice these roles may overlap or fuse and a contribution in any one area may come from any individual. They all aim to serve the teacher-users. We conclude this section by identifying in more detail the tasks that each of the named roles implies.

15

Curriculum designer

The curriculum designer has the job of seeing the unit through its various stages from the initial discussion and the selection of the teaching aims and content of the unit to its more detailed specification and drafting, the production of a draft program and teaching notes, its classroom development, editing and publication. He is both the producer and director and should be centrally involved in all the creative aspects of the work, except those which are technical (such as programming and graphic design). In this he should be fully aware of the options available. He is involved in all four development loops. He has both management (M) and educational (E) tasks including the following:

M — identify members of the group
M — organize regular meetings
M — consult with the group to draw up timetable
M — organize observations in classroom
E — collate the observations
E — consult with group in drawing inferences from observation data
E — take responsibility for decision on final changes
M — liaise with publishers
E — organize and possibly write documentation of new material
M — organize editing and rewriting of material
E — assume major role in the restrospective evaluation of the unit.

In order to carry out these tasks he may need to

— consult with subject specialist
— consult with teachers
— consult with computer specialists.

Apart from the program designer, teacher developers and teacher users, the curriculum designer will need to enlist the help of observers and editors. Help of trained observers and a trained editor cannot be overrated.

Program designer

The program designer takes charge of the production of the computer program for the unit which must achieve a presentation that allows the educational objectives to be reached. A further paper (see reference 10) discusses in more detail the problems of the step-by-step development of a program.

The program designer needs to be in communication with the curriculum designer, especially at the very beginning of the development. Chapter 2 should help him keep a firm eye on the educational objectives at a time when the technical challenge will tend to dominate his thoughts.

Apart from working on the teaching unit which is under development he will need to keep very well informed about new techniques in programming, new hardware, etc. If the development of the unit spans a long period it will be essential to make use of new developments of this kind.

Teacher developer
The teacher developers are distinguished from the teacher users by the fact that they must already be well acclimatized to using computers in the classroom. At the first stages of development they will be asked to take first draft programs into the classroom, maybe even in the form of sub-programs. Information from these initial trials will be extremely useful to the designers. Indeed the curriculum designer, the program designer and the teacher developers all need to be, as far as possible, 'computer literate', 'observer literate', 'subject literate', in other words they should be able to communicate clearly about all aspects of the work. They will play a very full role in revision of both programs and published documents.

Teacher user
Teacher users, as termed in this taxonomy, are the teachers who use the teaching unit when it is already well through its initial development stages. They are more or less in the position that teachers will be when they receive the published item. Thus the teacher users will be teaching the whole system — program plus published documents. It is advisable that a good cross-section of teachers play this role and that they are not really involved in the initial stages of development in order that the ultimate effectiveness of the unit can be assessed. It is this stage of trials that can be quite lengthy as teachers need to be able to try out material at a suitable place in the curriculum. Skimping on the classroom trials is almost certain to produce inferior results.

Observers and editors
We consider the task of the observer is one that requires much discussion with the group of designers of the materials. We shall consider methods of observation in detail in Chapter 3.

The editor's role is one that is very time-consuming and tedious but it demands good critical evaluation as well as sharp observation of consistency of presentation. To identify somebody with such skills and sufficient knowledge of the subject matter who also has the time and energy to take on the task will be a major problem to most groups.

As both these jobs are difficult and time-consuming they tend to get neglected until the final part of the development, which is a great pity.

We have identified the separate *roles* which are important in the design and development process. When many of these are taken by *one person* it is still useful for him or her to ensure that the separate responsibilities are kept in balance — and essential if the work is to be of use to other teachers.

2. Teaching style and program design

On getting ideas

Where do the good ideas come from and how can you know that your idea is worth pursuing? As with any creative work there can be no prescription that will guarantee a fund of good teaching ideas. Group discussions in which ideas are freely generated in an atmosphere where criticism is deferred ('brain-storming'), the careful review of ideas and material in related areas and other media, the organization and observation of 'happenings' indirectly linked to the questions of interest — these are some of the well-known suggestions for generating ideas. It may also help to set out some educational objectives against which the ideas will be tested; these will channel the search into the area of interest.

These objectives will vary from one designer to another and you will need to decide for yourself what your own priorities are. For example, as it is very time-consuming to produce a teaching unit, one approach would be only to accept an idea if it could produce a unit that:

(i) can be used by a wide range of teachers whose style of teaching varies a great deal
(ii) can be of use to a wide age-range of pupils
(iii) can be of use to a wide ability-range of pupils
(iv) can encourage work on concepts as well as on content
(v) may be of use in more than one subject discipline
(vi) is suitable for demonstration mode with a large class
(vii) is suitable for small groups or individuals to use
(viii) can be used to produce further teaching materials
(ix) can be used in teacher-training.

This list of requirements might well succeed in eliminating all our ideas; in practice we would be satisfied if two or three of these demands were catered for but very unhappy with a unit that failed on all nine aspects.

Most good ideas come from working towards a target. For example, suppose you are clear that you are trying:

— to introduce teachers of English in secondary schools to the microcomputer and show them its potential as an aid to their teaching objectives, and
— to produce a teaching unit that will generate a great deal of hypothesising and discussion amongst the children.

It is from the people who gather together to discuss these targets that ideas to meet them might well emerge. A quite different group would gather if your objectives were:

— to show children that mathematics can be fun, and
— to develop the skill of graph interpretation.

From such a discussion, the three elements of STORYLINE gradually emerged. Another target that one designer is pursuing is 'screen animation in geometry as a means of getting children to *say* what they *see*'. When such a clear target has been voiced and accepted, ideas for units begin to flow at a rate which the technology and the programmer find difficult to cope with. In all cases it could still be wise to check back against the nine more general objectives that were stated earlier and also refer to the draft checklist 1 (page 85).

The high standards aimed at in such a sifting process are important if we want teachers to go to the trouble of organizing the use of our materials in their teaching. For the foreseeable future, units involving the microcomputer as a teaching aid can only contribute to a very small proportion of curriculum time — at present certainly no more than a few hundred hours out of about 50,000 hours of 'different' teaching in the school curriculum for ages 5 to 18. We therefore want units that bring something qualitatively new, and valuable for most classrooms — an aspect of in-service education, if you like.

It may be best to try to specify the teaching objectives in behavioural terms — planning the thoughts and particularly the *activities* that you envisage for the pupils and the teacher. Our natural tendency to concentrate on what the program does and what appears on the screen can easily leave the class in the role of passive spectators, with exercises added almost as an afterthought. Concentrating on objectives for pupil activity will lead to the selection of different ideas and to units which surprise by what they leave out. (PIRATES is a unit on coordinates that never plots a point or shows a grid or axes. JANE requires you to guess at and check a set of mathematical functions without ever giving you the answers.)

A final comment, to move right to the other end of the production process. Once a unit has been written towards clearly defined aims (or 'intentions' in philosopher's language) it can be used to promote thought about the relationship between these aims and the behaviour that results in practice. The micro, which is itself able to display rich patterns of behaviour, perhaps presents us with these opportunities for the first time. A teaching unit must be capable of expressing the teacher's, possibly shifting, aims — just as a spade expresses the gardener's. We have to have several different kinds of spade to do this successfully — hence the features of ITMA units.

In summing up on this ideas section, we seem to be moving towards advocating that you:

(i) fix on some aims or targets or intentions
(ii) decide how these might relate to the actions and behaviour of pupils and teachers
(iii) try to produce a teaching unit that is illustrative of these intentions and that strives towards promoting some of the desired behaviour
(iv) report back on the actual relationship between the intentions and the behaviour.

The ideas will arise from the identification of (i) and (ii) and the development will be affected by the intentions expressed; (iii) and (iv) will help to educate us towards tuning the materials and producing other effective teaching units. All this is summarized in the figure below. However, we conclude as we began by repeating that there are no 'golden rules' for producing good ideas.

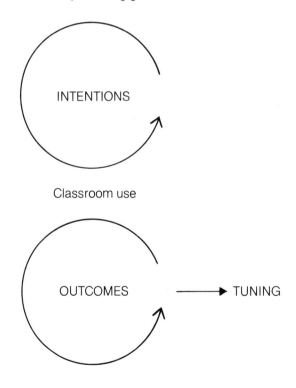

INTENTIONS

Classroom use

OUTCOMES   ⟶   TUNING

Program design variables

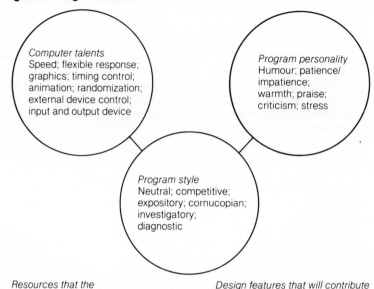

Computer talents
Speed; flexible response;
graphics; timing control;
animation; randomization;
external device control;
input and output device

Program personality
Humour; patience/
impatience;
warmth; praise;
criticism; stress

Program style
Neutral; competitive;
expository; cornucopian;
investigatory;
diagnostic

Resources that the
computer offers

Design features that will contribute
to the teaching environment

We now attempt to produce a taxonomy of some variables of program design and use which we believe are important in creating effective curriculum material. We discuss the computer program in rather anthropomorphic terms, referring successively to the *talents, personality* and *style* of the computer program. For different teaching styles and situations certain combinations of these variables may prove more effective than others. The list is presented mainly to alert the design team to the many dimensions that it is possible to work in.

Notes on computer talents
Speed. The speed of information processing of computers, allowing thousands, even millions of operations per second, underlies many of their potential capabilities. Programs can involve much more elaborate calculations than the teacher, let alone the pupils, can possibly undertake in the class; equally the management of information to appear on the screen is essentially sophisticated. The program may simply do quite normal calculations for the teacher, thus freeing his attention for other matters in the classroom. *However, it is not difficult to demand a speed of calculation beyond the performance of currently available microcomputers and teaching programs can easily provoke awkward pauses while the class waits for a calculation to be completed.*

Graphics. The ability to display information in the form of characters, including both numbers and letters, graphs of various kinds and even crude pictures, is one of the most powerful talents that the micro possesses. The impact of the television screen is very compelling and it is the graphics facilities of the computer system that enables the program designer to utilize it. We shall not attempt a complete classification of the different possibilities for using graphics but simply give a few examples and point out some general possibilities and dangers. The graphics facilities allow the teacher to develop pictures with far more control than the blackboard or even the overhead projector normally provides. The advantage for static illustrations is less important than the dynamic qualities that arise from the interactive role of the microcomputer. The drawing of graphs and diagrams are obvious examples, but simpler possibilities such as the creation of large characters and simple block diagrams may have an even greater psychological impact in the classroom. Not only Cartesian graphs but contour plots and maps can also be effective.

We have stressed the paramount importance of pupil activity and *the designer must guard against the danger that the sophisticated graphics possibilities of the micro may actually undermine the development of the pupils' skills in drawing and interpreting graphs and other diagrams.*

Thorough understanding of the impact of visual presentations is not a normal part of training of teachers and other academics, and care is needed to ensure that the effect in the classroom is actually what was intended; there is no substitute for classroom experiment in this area. Also, current computer systems and their software often limit the effective use of the screen unless the designer is ingenious enough to overcome such limitations. Professional advice on graphic design is valuable.

Animation. Together with the ability to respond interactively, animation allows the designer to produce more vitality in the image the program presents to the user. Although the speed of the computer does not allow animation comparable to that which can be produced on film, there is no doubt that this facility, which has only just begun to be explored, can give real power to the teacher. *Again, there is a danger that pleasure in exploiting this new tool may cause the designer to lose sight of the educational objectives of the program.*

External device control. Apart from the usual output media of the screen and the printer the micro could be used to control a wide variety of external devices from a simple bell through a slide or film projector to various forms of apparatus or even robots. The effectiveness of the micro in simulating experiments hinges on the children's accepting the analogy with the true experimental situation. This can be established by programs in which the actual experimental apparatus is linked to a computer simulation. A pendulum would provide a simple example. This approach also provides a direct illustration of one major application of microprocessors in process control. However, the complications involved in setting up micro-linked experiments are such that they should only be used when the educational profit is clear.

Input and output devices. At the present time, the keyboard, screen and printer remain the dominant devices for communicating with the computer, with tape and disc as the principal storage facilities. However, there is little doubt that a number of facilities already developed will prove of value educationally: devices which allow the user effectively to draw upon the screen, such as the light pen or the graphics tablet, have great potential. Voice input and output offer possibilities which are only beginning to be explored. All of these are still very cumbersome to use at the present stage of development but there is no doubt that they will improve. That they have an important role to play is already clear in certain areas, such as special education. Keyboards designed to meet the needs of the physically handicapped are already being developed.

A flexible response. The designer can program the computer to respond in any way to a chosen input stimulus. This obvious fact is not always exploited — there is a tendency to regard the keyboard simply as a typewriter whereas any key can be chosen to have any function. Equally, an area on a graphics tablet can form an extremely flexible form of control; for example, a diagram could be laid over such a tablet — the user could then see clearly all the control possibilities and by touching the correct part of the diagram he could control the program with ease.

Timing control. This allows the designer to plan the way in which the user will interact with the program in real time. *There is evidence of the importance of timing in stimulating pupil learning.* The micro will allow this both to be used and further explored. (This is but one aspect of the possibilities of the micro as a research tool in education, a subject of importance which we shall discuss further elsewhere.)

Randomization. We believe that the computer's ability to generate quasi-random numbers is educationally most important. Obviously it allows the production of a very large number of exercise examples.

But the psychological possibilities are more interesting. A randomly produced example leaves the teacher 'on the same side as' the pupils. Questions set by the computer, which then supplies the answer for checking purposes after a randomly set time delay, seem to have a powerful motivating effect and are but one example of the effectiveness of the computer's simulating the random elements which the pupil experiences in everyday life and work. The class list of children's names can be in the program together with a set of comments — the random selection of child plus a comment, eg, 'Wake up Hilary', certainly keeps the class on its toes.

Notes on program personality
The program personality presented to the student, and to the teacher, need not be that of a neutral machine — it can show a variety of human attributes, and the balancing of these in the design of the program is an important matter in which there is room for a variety of approaches. In our experience, the extremes of neutrality ('response incorrect') and folksiness ('aw,c'mon') are equally likely to alienate the student.

Humour epitomizes the designer's dilemma — used effectively it can prolong the attention span of the students and enhance the whole atmosphere of the class, but *it needs to be used with a very light touch* if, particularly after using the program many times, disenchantment is to be avoided.

Warmth of program image is an asset to be sought in a variety of ways. A facility, as mentioned before, for using the actual names of the children in the class (input in advance by the teacher) can be effective. *Fundamentally, the program must present the demands it makes on the class as worthwhile, achievable and, preferably, enjoyable.*

Praise and *criticism* are obvious parts of any interactive teaching material, but the balance must be carefully adjusted both in the initial design and the classroom development of the program unit. The value of praise in providing encouragement has to be blended with the instructional benefit that criticism can bring to the pupil. We believe there is room for experiment in this area in particular. *Eventual guaranteed success is often a very desirable aspect, especially for young or slow learners.*

Stress can easily be generated in a class by a teaching program, through the use of competitive situations, for example. It can be used to obtain responses from pupils beyond what they would otherwise achieve. However, undue pressure may result in actual distress for some pupils and, much more likely, a general rejection of the program by the class. Stress can also be placed on the teacher by careless program design or careless program use. During the use of some programs, eg, PIRATES (see reference 1), if the pace of the lesson is not controlled, so much information is contained in pupil responses and computer responses that it is almost impossible for the teacher to process it as efficiently as he would like.

Patience and *impatience* are one of the key ways in which the pressure that the program puts upon pupils can be adjusted. Control of the rhythm of the lesson will depend partly on the structure of the program and how easy it is for the teacher to use.

Notes on program style
Program style is obviously related to how the teacher and program operate together to create the total learning environment — this is also discussed in the next section on classroom activities. We are concerned with the micro being used with a class of children or a group of children. Observing in the classroom, we have been very encouraged to see that many programs that were originally designed and written to be used with a whole class (maybe as many as 30 pupils participating) are very effective with groups of pupils working on their own, either with the same approach taken with the whole class or with a subset of the possible activities offered by the program being tackled (eg, PIRATES, JANEPLUS and TRANSPOTS). In the same way, material written for the individual child is often being used with one child operating the keyboard and a group of children involved. In all situations the communication between pupils themselves and between pupils and teachers appears to increase.

Interactive computer programs can present in a powerful way ideas, facts and basic techniques. It can aim for their assimilation and the development of conceptual understanding of the more strategic skills. Exercise and testing play an important part at all levels. Program design can aim to aid any or all these activities by:

– actual presentation: sowing seeds
– generating a supportive environment: producing curiosity or other motivation in an atmosphere of enjoyment
– stimulating pupil participation: in setting up situations or exploiting them, providing a structure for investigations, examples or exercises.

The following program styles at least are available; a single program may employ more than one.

Neutral. The micro is used simply as a device for presenting information as requested by the teacher — an electronic variant of the blackboard or overhead projector which uses the computer's talents, for example, to do graphs, display pictures, record and reproduce data, or perform calculations.

Expository. The program 'teaches' a topic itself, presenting ideas in a straightforward didactic way and initiating pupil activity with specific tasks. The teacher's role is mainly managerial and supportive in this mode.

Investigatory. The program provides a system for the teacher to explore with the class. Computer *simulations* of physical or social systems are the best-known examples of this mode, but the possibilities are much wider. *In particular, programs which illustrate theoretical concepts directly in numerical, graphical or symbolic terms can provide a powerful 'bridge' in the development of abstract concepts.* The teacher's role here in providing the right amount of guidance in the investigation is most important, with room for wide differences of approach, particularly on the levels of demand to be placed on the pupil.

Competitive environments have a powerful stimulant effect on a class. *The swift interactive response of the micro and its flexibility within a well-defined set of rules make it particularly effective in setting up game situations.* Its data-holding potential allows it to be used to help ensure that all pupils are involved in the game as well as the traditional competitive classroom activity, testing. The optimum use of the micro in these ways needs further research.

Cornucopian. The prolific production of examples (which is an essential element of the investigatory style) can also be used to provide a multitude of practice exercises. The polishing of basic technical skills in this way is well known; but more work is needed to learn how to provide good problems for the development of higher-level problem-solving skills in all subject areas.

Diagnostic. Although it is possible when a program is used for individual tuition for it to collect data on pupil performance, this is only one mode of diagnostics. Indeed this mode should be used with care as it may well be the non-judgemental personality of a machine that motivates a child to persevere with a problem. We have observed in the classroom that many programs help the teacher to understand the pupils' level of comprehension through the pupil response that they provoke. The observations so far are with programs where the designer had not concentrated on this aspect at all, but it seems very hopeful that valuable work in this area can be developed.

Program in action
The influence of teaching material on what happens in the classroom has usually been overrated. Writers of textbooks have a clear view of what they are trying to achieve, and, encouraged by their own success when developing the material, too easily believe that other teachers will use it in the same way when guided only by a well-written instruction, or even just the 'clear' implication of style in the material itself. However, detailed observations of a variety of teachers using the same material (see, for example, reference 2) immediately reveals the wide range of teaching styles that are used and the apparent ease with which almost any material can be absorbed into any style. This is normally accompanied by the equally widespread concentration on the factual content or the basic manipulative skills in the material and the associated neglect of the higher-level objectives that were probably the author's main motivation in developing it in the first place. *It is not easy for teachers significantly to change their style, so such demands should be severely limited and when they are made, a lot of help given. The program designer, in creating material of a much less familiar kind, needs a clear view of how the teaching unit may be used by a variety of teachers and how he may help them use it effectively.* Such views will be modified in the light of the classroom development of program and its associated documentation. (We have evidence to suggest that program teaching units can be rather effective at showing teachers new teaching possibilities, including those involving style changes; nonetheless we reemphasize the dangers of including such demands.)

Teaching experience and observing other teachers is a tremendous help to the designer of educational software. To help this observation provide as much information as possible to the designer, we now give a simple discussion of a range of lesson activities. We consider how a computer program could support them, also what balance of teacher, pupil and program interaction might prove effective. The text is based on ideas that have been developed through observations and trials in the classroom — they are offered in the spirit of exploration rather than in supplying definitive answers to the designer's problems. The teaching checklist 3 in the Appendix epitomizes some of the issues he faces.

Whilst reading the following paragraphs keep an eye on checklist 2, and also consider the program personality headings together with program style suggestions, as decisions about these will influence the presentation of the content of the lesson and affect the environment finally created in the classroom. Finally, we have found it salutary to remember that teachers will use the program in quite different ways and it is they who will manage and build the total activity. We assume in this section that the program offers the teacher adequate flexibility, ie, the various routes must be easily accessible from the program control. On page 35 we consider this problem of teacher/program interface in detail.

Introducing a new section of work or new topic
In this activity the teacher will want, among other things to:

(a) set the scene
(b) capture attention and focus interest in the topic
(c) check that the previous work this section depends on is adequately remembered or understood
(d) cater for the levels of activity of the pupils.

Setting the scene and capturing attention are more easily assisted by a computer program than the other aims. The use of animated graphics can focus attention; an investigatory program style that encourages a high level of pupil participation will arouse interest and possibly a healthy curiosity about the new work. Checking of previous work without the teacher asking too many questions could be helped by a program written in a game environment. The game could also provide links to the new topic by various levels of play providing a variety of challenges. The information that the pupil responses give the teacher is often surprising and considerable and certainly extremely helpful in ascertaining the depth of knowledge and understanding the children have reached.

The fourth aim of catering for the different levels of ability is more likely to be teacher-dependent. Often quite different language and notations are needed with different groups; it would be a very ambitious program that attempted to cope with this. *We feel that it is much better to recognize clearly that some roles should be the teacher's province and that the program designer should not try to employ the program in such roles.* Care should thus be taken that the program itself should not dictate language or notation levels except under teacher control.

Summing up, it appears that good bold graphics and a variety of visual presentations of the new topic offer strong support to the teacher at this stage. In the humanities, a rich databank with an easy-to-use retrieval system would offer a great deal, either in illustration or, particularly, for an exploratory approach. The teacher's role may well and probably should be the major one with computer programs providing plenty of illustrations and challenges.

Exercising a topic or skill
Time spent practising skills, learning facts, and doing exercises is needed to allow understanding of concepts and knowledge to grow by experience and observation. Time and practice can be the essence of development and each child's requirements will tend to be different from its neighbour's. It seems that individual work with some group work is often beneficial, and we can certainly turn to the computer to provide some material. Using randomization, it is possible to generate many examples of a similar nature that, if required, can also be self-grading against pupil performance.

Again, environments that make exercising entertaining can be employed, perhaps including some competitive element such as a game or simply a timed response system. One program, AUTOFRACTIONS (see reference 3), that has been used very successfully in the classroom produces large fractions on the screen in the format $^4/_{15} = {}^?/_{60}$, with the ? appearing in one of the four positions each time. The program runs continuously in 'film mode' but at the beginning the teacher sets the level of difficulty and the time-delay before the correct answer appears; a sequence of randomly generated fractions follows. Children seem to be highly motivated by this 'beat the computer' situation with its immediate feedback system. For this type of activity the 'film type' program can provide what is needed for a whole class with little teacher intervention. The computer program will dominate at such times and promote considerable activity; the teacher is then free to concentrate on management and coaching activities, and a discussion of tactics.

Interactive exercises and off-line exercises are both possibilities. Indeed both types can be generated from a program that provides an introduction to or an investigation of a topic. An advantage of this technique is that the teacher can decide while using the program what level of exercises to generate — the computer program offers a great deal more flexibility in this respect than an ordinary textbook. Two programs that provide this sort of service are JANEPLUS and TRANSPOTS (see references 4 and 5).

Progression through a topic
This is discussed under five subheadings.

(a) Differential progress for different pupil ability will be needed as the progression proceeds. This demand for flexibility will tend to swing the balance of load back to the teacher, with the computer program in a supportive role. It can certainly provide help with specific difficulties

such as sustaining different activities for groups that are at opposite ends of the ability range. Computer talents such as selective input, timing, randomization, patience, diagnostic design, are useful. With a group or a class responding and interacting with each other, the teacher's skill in interpreting and reacting immediately are all-important. It is through the driving system that the flexibility of program use is obtained. *However, we need to identify what specific form of flexibility is of use to the teacher under different circumstances.* Here the teacher needs the ability to call on different levels of presentation — graded illustrations or examples or maybe graded presentations from pictures through to other more abstract notations. Diagnostics (see page 32) have a role to play — perhaps where individual computer use is possible, diagnostics for the child's consumption only would be beneficial.

It may well be more effective for the program not to attempt anything too complicated and for the teacher to provide and guide the questions at the level required.

(b) Linking together the most important elements and providing memory aids. Helping the teacher with this most important activity places great demands on the program designer from both the curriculum and the presentation viewpoint. In no area is there a greater need for a rich variety of creative ideas. Each teacher tends to have his own particular strategy and will wish to employ the computer program as part of it. Careful build-up of specific links, starting with concentration on one or two connected facts and building up to a complex structure, could be provided by a program — such a program may even have the potential of becoming a generalized structure.

Memory aids identified by the teacher, particularly useful in the build-up of a topic, could be given special treatment in program presentation, using such computer talents as graphics, colour and animation and the 'personal attribute' of humour to emphasize and help retention. Games, simulation and competition environments could be well employed at this stage.

(c) Deeper understanding by examination of different presentations of the same ideas. One major block to progress that is created in mathematics is the constant use of a single notation to represent a concept: for example, always labelling a triangle ABC, always using only Cartesian coordinates (x, y) in representing points. Of course, consistency in notation builds up a certain level of skill with that notation, but it is vitally important to develop skills at least partially independent of a single notation. Program flexibility could assist the

teacher deliberately to build up more secure understanding. Different presentations of situations would be very effective on the screen and it would be possible to control the display with ease. *This problem is certainly not restricted to mathematics and the program designer and teaching team should consider very carefully the various presentations they would like to have available.* For any topic being taught, a full communication system needs to be developed giving the student as wide and varied a vocabulary as possible.

(d) Motivation to persist. This is perhaps the most vital subheading. The teacher now needs all the possible aids at his disposal. In conjunction with the teacher, examination of all the computer talents is needed by the program designer. Serious consideration of the design style should take place. The game environment, competitive elements and display and presentation purely directed at enjoyment can be very effective in capturing attention. *A major consideration for the teacher is to ensure accessible success experiences for the majority of the pupils; this again can be achieved at varying levels with a carefully tuned balance between demands from the teacher and demands from the program.*

(e) Diagnosis of remedial needs. Since this must be done on an individual basis, the interplay with the teacher must be sensitively planned, with accommodation for the full range of teaching styles. In its simplest use, the computer sits in a corner and each child has an individual session with relevant material; so inevitably only a short time would normally be available. Small groups could also operate in this way with the teacher matching or mismatching the ability of the group, according to the strategy of learning aimed at.

As mentioned previously, it is probably unwise to build stand-alone diagnostic systems that are independent of teacher-control. The designer and teacher need to discuss the level of diagnostic help program support may supply. Again it is important that the machine does not assume a 'big brother' role.

Revision of topics
We discuss this under three subheadings.

(a) Linking up the threads of the topic or even several topics together.
This complex phase of learning, which requires the pupils to make a synthesis, really demands high-level skills from the teacher — the supporting role of the computer program can nevertheless be an

important one. Whether within a single topic or within a range of topics, the construction of material aimed to illustrate links between concepts or links between topics is a fascinating but demanding exercise. Indeed, it may very well be an area where some programs can be of immediate and wide-ranging use to teachers. The game environment can prove to be useful in providing the vehicle for this purpose. In the linking-up of the threads of the topic, the flexibility of the program may provide the gradual building-up of links so that the student has a chance to see the development from various angles.

The interaction across topics involves longer-range transfer and leads to the beginning of the exploration of problem-solving. A revision exercise set within an environment indicates which variables or considerations are pertinent, whereas in true problem-solving, the environment is less well defined and the identification of pertinent information is a difficult aspect of solution. Thus in this linking process, the teacher requires flexibility to help pupils build links at a speed with which they can cope.

(b) Test and practice in disguise. Flexibility here would be very similar to the exercising activities described above. However, the tests would be more wide-ranging and control of the number of different aspects under test at any one time would be useful.

(c) Provision of summary. Here a tree branching structure of control may allow the major items of the revision to be checked through. This type of program could provide a systematic approach to the game environment suggested in the other sections. The teacher would need to play a full role in the revision activity, monitoring and providing remedial help wherever necessary. We recognize that often revision has consisted simply of repetition of the same type of exercise that was used in learning the topic, but it is self-evident that effective revision must involve the synthesis with the assimilation of the new concepts and techniques by the pupil.

Problem-solving activities
Firstly, pupils need to identify the tools that they require in order to solve the problem, and they must then be able to manipulate the tools effectively. Often it is necessary to start activity with some contrived problems that restrict demand on the pupil, ie, only a narrow range of techniques and knowledge is involved, while the presentation level will depend on the group's ability. A program could allow the teacher to start at this level and offer as its flexibility the opportunity to introduce a random element into the problem and also to have varying levels of 'noise' fed in, so that we gradually move towards a

suitable environment for real problem-solving. Skills that pupils need in mathematics, for example, include:

- comprehension, and the enumeration of possibilities
- translation skills from words to numbers
- translation skills from numbers to graphs or equations
- creation of mathematical models of the problem

as well as more traditional mathematical skills now taught explicitly.

Teachers need to recognize problem-solving as a specific activity, build it into the curriculum — perhaps well-designed computer programs could assist this difficult task by creating some interesting environments which if not exactly 'real' can have some exciting behaviour to explore. In exploring such environments pupils will experience the type of argument and logical analysis that will prepare them for the real-life problems they will tackle outside.

Hypothesising and checking out are important activities. They can indeed be developed by quite simple computer environments, eg, JANEPLUS, by quite young children. Indeed computer aid may well open up many more problem-solving activities to younger children.

Teaching style
We shall not attempt here to give any detailed classification of teaching style. However, it is crucial to the successful design of programs for general use that the designer be aware of the wide variety of ways in which his material will be used — if it is used at all by others. We, in our observations so far of a number of teachers using the same program teaching units, have been more impressed by the disparity of the lessons than by their similarity. Although it was true in each case that the essential content was the same, the emphasis varied so much that the skills and concepts developed were essentially different.

In what dimensions do these differences lie? One teacher, for example, will structure the discussion very carefully so the pupils concentrate simply on getting the details right, while another may hand the whole problem to the class and then force them to justify any suggestions they make. (In the SCAN scheme of analysis — see reference 2 — which we have developed to provide feedback to curriculum designers on the use of their material, we call these 1 and 3 levels of teacher guidance respectively, the level of demand is similarly classified (α, β, γ). The classification has been found useful much more widely. The activity and episode checklists in the

Appendix are derived from SCAN). Equally, one teacher may concentrate on independent pupil investigations while another believes in clear explanation of principles and examples followed by closely imitative exercises. Other dimensions contrast theoretical with practical, descriptive with analytical, or factual with problem-solving approaches. Analyses of science teaching (see reference 6) have shown tendencies for the preferred style to be subject-dependent but with a great range within each subject. *The designer who assumes all teachers will teach like him, or as he intends, is probably writing private programs. To do better is not easy — but it is possible.*

Driving the program
The aims and potential objectives of the teaching unit will be built into the teaching material, the computer program being a part of this material, and their successful realization by a wide range of teachers will depend crucially on the driving system of the program and the image of the unit that it presents to the user. This should be at the centre of the designer's attention throughout the development of the unit — indeed, starting with preliminary ideas of what options the program should present to the user and then refining and extending them, the program will develop in tune with the feedback received from the classroom.

There is an inherent tension between range and flexibility of options on the one hand and their simplicity and clarity on the other. It has several aspects, including:

(a) the range of options offered to the teacher is crucial in fitting the program to his style and enabling him to contribute effectively, but too many will be confusing
(b) the designer may see a whole range of possible extensions to the teaching possibilities of the program: the lengthy development process of all good teaching units makes such extensions attractive but trying to include them in one program will tend to make it difficult to 'see through' and to use
(c) the desire for compatibility with different hardware configurations often inspires programming constraints that can be severe; conversely, programs that fully exploit the facilities of a particular microcomputer are likely to be difficult to transfer.

In defining the program image and writing the documentation the designer has to draw a balance in all these dimensions, informed by development trials in the classroom. *It is important always to consider the probable roles of teacher, pupils and program to ensure that the partnership is a productive one.* Checklists are an aid towards this end.

The driving system, then, is crucial in making a program that will be effective in the hands of a lot of teachers. What elements are important in its design? The novice teacher will require careful guidance through the option structure of the program with clear explanations and very limited demands in terms of making choices, if he is not to be distracted from the normal demands of teaching or even put off completely. The more experienced teacher who has used the program several times, on the other hand, will not want to go through lengthy explanations and interrogations by the program amid the pressures of the classroom. He will be able to handle a wider range of options with only mnemonic guidance — for him the minimum number of key-strokes for program control is appropriate. It is our view that designers should generally pursue such an economical, even terse, style but with a clearly-defined choice structure, regarding 'initial training' as a separate task.

The best way to define the choice structure remains a matter of research. However, it is likely to be preferable to limit the range of choices facing the teacher at any moment and to group them in a natural way from a teaching point of view. Various sorts of logical structure, with branching and loops, will achieve this — in general we see great advantages in presenting them to the user in graphical form.

There are, of course, no unique prescriptions for realizing these principles but we think it worth examining a few possible approaches in a little more detail. The traditional form of interaction with the user is purely through dialogue in which written messages present him with immediately available choices, or ask him to supply values for parameters in the program; this approach has grown from individual tutorial CAI. It has the advantage that the user is given a feeling of security by being concerned only with a limited range of immediate decisions. There are at least two disadvantages from the class-use point of view. The lengthy explanatory messages required take time to read and absorb and are a potential distraction to the class. In addition (and this also applies to tutorial CAI) the user is given no help in forming a global picture of what the program can achieve.

The topological structure of the decision space can be quite complicated in even a fairly simple program. Such structures are best displayed graphically (even parliamentary draughtsmen have resorted to flowcharts for the definition of some more complex legislation). The drivecharts (see reference 7), which we have described fully elsewhere, are an example of this approach being specifically adapted to the sorts of decisions that are characteristic of a program used in class- or group-teaching. We shall outline their main features here.

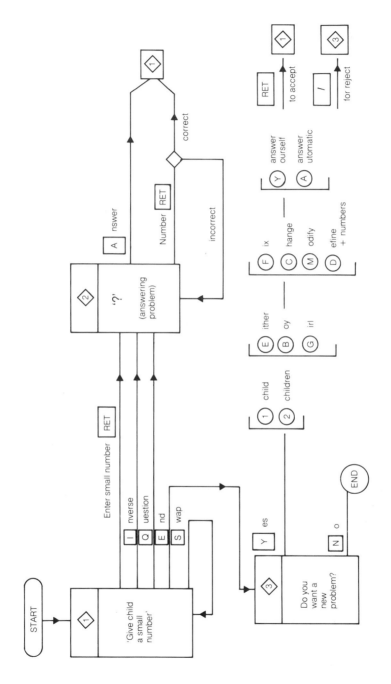

JANEPLUS drivechart

This figure shows the drivechart for the program JANEPLUS, which aims to introduce pupils to the idea of mathematical functions by displaying *named* figures, each of which either adds or multiplies by a particular small whole number — which number the pupils must discover by trial, hypothesis and check. On the drivechart the decision points, represented by square boxes, each offer a natural group of alternative routes to the teacher, who chooses one by pressing a single key — eg, 'I' selects the *inverse* problem where the computer provides the 'output' number from the named function and invites the class to guess the 'input' number. Along certain routes there is a 'menu' of features that may be set — one being chosen from each vertical group or 'course'. It is easy to see from this drivechart that the number of possible modes of operation is large, but that the choice facing the teacher at any given moment is among only a few possibilities. The global structure of choices is clearly displayed.

The price paid for this powerful system is the introduction of a new unfamiliar notation with its associated fear factor for many teachers, particularly those unused to mathematics or flowcharts. This is the 'initial training' problem referred to earlier. It can be met in various ways. The written material for the unit should contain a detailed guide to the drivechart, including keypress-by-keypress sequences to take the teacher through simple and commonly used options. Such training sequences can also be included as an optional part of the program, which should also contain 'help' routines to feed information to the teacher who is having difficulties. Such a training system has been found in practice to be very effective with a wide range of teachers.

Simpler systems are possible — for example, all the options in the program may be available at any time, and in certain circumstances this may be preferable. The price of this simple structure is that there is no framework to help the teacher make the choices from the large total number that is often in principle available. The balance between these factors needs further research.

The more complicated the decision space of the program, the more sophisticated will be the optimum driving system which may ultimately need most of the features of the full graphics-oriented database management system. Perhaps the most highly developed example currently available in an educational context is the DYNABOOK system developed by Adele Goldberg and others at Xerox's Palo Alto Research Center. Although this is designed for individual use, its flexibility and generality are such that it is seen as worth describing here. Written in the language SMALLTALK, it is designed to enable the user easily to produce, modify and recall graphical, textual and numerical information in a very flexible way.

Since the language is only recently published and is not yet implemented on any commercially available computer system (Apple 4 when it is available may support a subset of the SMALLTALK) (see reference 8), we shall not try to describe its structural syntax but only some of its essential elements. A *window* is a screen display stored in the computer which can be created, recalled, modified, scaled, repositioned and combined or overlapped with other windows by user *messages*. These are commands selected from menus displayed on the screen — although the keyboard is used, the main input device is currently the 'mouse' which when moved on a table produces corresponding movements of a pointer arrow on the screen. High-quality graphics allow much more detail to be displayed, and thus more choices offered, than a touchscreen or lightpen system can currently provide. A button on the mouse 'sends' the messages. A 'browsing' system allows the user to explore the whole direction of facilities, organized as a 'tree', including the SMALLTALK language itself. This system is suitable only for highly sophisticated programmers, but it has been used to assemble 'kits' of teaching material from which various teaching packages can be built by the teacher-user.

We regard it as unlikely that many teachers in the near future will be able to handle facilities of this range and power amid the pressures of the classroom. However, it is important for the designer to be aware of the nature and extent of the possibilities that are in principle available so that he may be able to exploit some of them when it seems appropriate.

In drawing this essential balance between flexibility and simplicity, the drive system checklist 4 in the appendix may be of value.

Programming considerations
The designer of a teaching unit involving a microcomputer must be aware that the available hardware and software facilities impose bounds, under each of the headings under 'Notes on computer talents' (page 22), upon the material which can be *successfully* implemented. *It is extremely easy to exceed these bounds when specifying a program, and so it is essential that a programmer experienced in the particular system or systems to be used is involved in the initial design discussions.* A fuller discussion of these issues is given in *Aspects of Programming for Teaching Unit Design and Development* by Colin Wells, to be published by the Council for Educational Technology.

At the initial design stage, and during the implementation of the program, the programmer needs to be aware of and act upon a number of factors.

The type of system used

The first thing to decide is the particular make (or makes) of hardware and software to be used for the implementation. Factors influencing this choice could be:

(a) the availability of the system to the programmer
(b) the availability of special hardware or software features on a particular machine which are necessary to the program
(c) the availability of the system (or a compatible system) in schools.

The last of these must be the overriding consideration; it would be of little use to develop a unit on an unusual system not readily available to the target population in schools, and not likely to be available in the near future. The choice of a system because of particular or peculiar features also needs careful consideration, as this implies that programs developed on such a system will be machine-dependent and not transferable to other systems. In this situation, it is worth comparing in detail the advantages of continuing the development of the unit exactly as required but on a limited range of systems, as against modifying the design so that it can be implemented on a wider range. In choosing systems the following features must be considered:

— make of computer
— version of ROM monitor, and of the operating system
— version of BASIC and its facilities, and other language alternatives
— amount of memory available for a user program
— availability of disc storage for files
— availability of cassette storage for files
— availability of additional hardware, eg, high-resolution graphics, sound generator, graphics tablets or voice control.

In all cases, educational desirability must be balanced against practicality and system availability, and these restrictions may be so severe as to result in the rejection of the design idea.

Range of facilities
A significant part of screening a design idea for practicality involves knowing the kinds of facilities or 'computer talents' that are realistically available as building blocks. Facilities could be considered in three categories:

(a) those provided by the 'standard' hardware and 'standard' system software

(b) those which can be obtained by modifying or extending the system software — but which will run on a 'standard' hardware system
(c) those which require special additional hardware.

The facilities available in each division will obviously depend on the particular system, but a fairly common division would be as follows.

(a) 'Standard' hardware and software 'abilities':
(i) evaluation of expressions involving simple arithmetic, exponential, trigonometric, logarithmic or logical functions in a reasonable time
(ii) manipulation of text
(iii) control over the positioning and layout of output on the screen
(iv) input of numbers or text by the user during a program run
(v) reading of numeric or text data during a program run which had been previously stored
(vi) branching to one course of action out of two possibilities depending upon the result of a mathematical, textual or logical condition
(vii) branching to one of a series of actions depending on a numeric value
(viii) repetition of a closed loop containing a series of instructions for a fixed number of values in an arithmetic sequence
(ix) generation of a series of pseudo-random numbers
(x) plotting of low-resolution graphics blocks in any order on a screen grid of (say) 80 by 50
(xi) modification of certain absolute memory locations in the machine — this allows the possibility of adding extra software facilities
(xii) control over input and output ports — this allows the possibility of adding extra hardware.

Although, at first sight, these look fairly primitive 'abilities', the fact that a microcomputer can obey quickly a large number of instructions consisting of a combination of these features enables most of the 'talents' described on page 22 to be made available. The main areas of restriction are due to the machine's inability or difficulty in coping with very large calculations at a satisfactory speed, large amounts of text or graphics, fast animation or large shapes, device control, and real-time control.

(b) Extra software abilities:
(i) the speeding up of routines which would otherwise be too slow and impractical to be used: this is particularly significant in the area of graphics where large figures can be produced at a good speed and some reasonably large-scale movement becomes possible

(ii) the addition of extra facilities not generally available in BASIC: for example, different forms of character input instruction, including timing, displaying a pre-stored picture 'instantly', and automatic device initialization (see next section).

Such additions to the software, which are necessarily written in machine code, are very effective but their production is fairly complex and time-consuming and can also lead to serious problems if transfer to a different machine is attempted. However, on a given range of machines the necessary additional routines can be installed and linked by the program which requires them (ie, the teaching unit program), so such programs can be run with standard software on standard systems, with the added complexity being transparent to the user.

(c) Extra hardware abilities:
(i) the addition of extra hardware boards or components in the computer can, with suitable software, provide such things as fast floating-point arithmetic — (making calculations significantly faster), medium- or high-resolution graphics up to a grid of (say) 500 by 500 points, sound and voice synthesis, colour output, a real-time clock, and standard device controllers. Many will become 'standard' soon.

These internal hardware additions are of course very machine-dependent, and those available vary considerably from manufacturer to manufacturer. Perhaps the least standardized range of facilities are those provided for high-resolution graphics, where not only is the grid size used different, but the forms of storage and manipulation provided are unique to the particular machine. If suitable machines are chosen, these graphics facilities can include such things as multiple pages and views (thus allowing very rapid animation of a short sequence of pictures), a large number of shades or colours to be used in one display (thus allowing effects of shading, shadow and three dimensions to be shown), shades on the screen 'instantly' changeable to any of a large range of 'colours' available, and superimposition of two different graphic views, low-resolution graphics and text.

(ii) The addition of 'standard' devices can also provide many extra abilities. The most common additional device is the cassette recorder, which allows a limited form of input and storage of data files, though this feature is provided much more quickly and efficiently by disc units. These devices in effect increase the size of program which can be run on a given machine, because much of the required data can be stored externally until needed. Other useful devices include printers to provide printed text or perhaps graphics as well, voice input, joystick controls, as well as graphics tablets, touch keyboards and light pens enabling flexible touch input and 'freehand' drawing input. There are simplified keyboards for young children.

Again, these are very dependent on the particular machine, but if used sensibly, and not just as gimmicks, they can completely transform a program.

(iii) The addition of non-standard do-it-yourself devices can obviously provide a wide range of spectacular additional facilities, but (except in the unlikely event of the program designers and programmers being in a position to market the additional hardware device with the program) the use of such devices is impractical for any program intended for use in a range of establishments.

A large microcomputer system with an extensive range of hardware devices and large block of extra machine-code routines is very flexible and powerful, and would go a long way to meeting the requirements of the program designer, but in realistic terms such a system would be too expensive for most schools at present. If all its facilities were used it would also cause too many problems of transfer to other systems. Therefore, at present, it is wise to design to work with systems which are likely to be available in schools in the near future, though options requiring extra facilities may sometimes be explored.

Performance of the program
The programmer of a unit must be aware of techniques for producing a program performance that will be acceptable to the user. In particular this means providing foolproof error-checking routines and positive help messages when required. The input to a program should be clear and kept to a minimum; the output on the screen should be clear and presented at a sensible speed; and any 'special' or complex computer procedures should appear to the user as ordinary and easy to use. Another very important area requiring care is that of adequate speed for complex routines; it may be necessary to sacrifice other ideals of structure, memory-size and transferability in order to make the performance right, and this *must* take priority. Particular examples of speed problems were given in the previous part of this section.

Internal efficiency of the program
With the limited memory and speed of a microcomputer, internal efficiency of the program code is very important. Efficiency could be

measured in terms of speed of performance, the least amount of storage required or the least number of program lines. *The programmer has to be aware right from the initial design stage of the implications of the program design in terms of memory and speed requirements, and must be aware of techniques for optimizing any combination of these factors that is required.*

Structure and readability of the program
Though not absolutely essential for a first draft version of a program, it is very important for later versions to be logically structured and easily readable so that they can be easily understood and modified by the author and others if required. Note that this may conflict with requirements of efficiency given above − for example, a chain of subroutines takes longer to obey than the expanded code and the liberal use of remark statements to aid readability uses up a lot of valuable memory. Here, performance and practicality may have to take precedence. Several conventions have been created to aid readability and structure, ranging from the use of particular variable names, through the fixing of line numbers for types of routines, to the use of prepared 'standard' routines from a 'library'. These are useful if they have been constructed flexibly enough to allow for complex unusual facilities to be used if required, and thus do not negate their advantage by imposing restrictions on the designers and programmers. Structure should be built in from the beginning.

Documentation of the program
As well as good documentation and 'driving' information for the user, as described on page 35, it is also very important to document the computer program as a further aid to those who wish to understand how the program works or modify it in some way. Obviously a well-structured program is easier to document as each subroutine should contain a logical element of the program, rather than the jumbled interconnected logic of an unstructured program. In particular, any special or complex routine, or routine involving additional software routines in machine code or hardware devices, should be explained in great detail. Documentation, too, is best built in as you go along.

Portability and transferability
Portability and transferability of programs between different systems is a considerable problem if any but the simplest facilities are used in a program. In particular, programs using graphics or requiring additional software routines or hardware devices will be difficult in this respect, and the programmer must cater for any intended transfer from the outset by establishing common features such as a

compatible screen grid-size and compatible device characteristics. Then all machine-dependent routines must be written as separate subroutines, with clear documentation, so that equivalent routines for another machine can be exchanged for them. *The programmer must, however check that the equivalent routine performs adequately as well as theoretically doing the same function.*

The seven items outlined above thus form a very important part of the design stage of a program, as well as in its implementation, as it is at this initial stage that the appropriate facilities and practicalities are planned.

3. Feedback from the classroom — principles and kits

Collecting information

Once the teaching unit has reached the stage of a draft computer program which does what the designer intends, together with associated notes which describe what the program offers and its possible uses in the classroom, we need to consider in more detail how to collect essential information as to what actually happens when the unit is used. How we collect this information will certainly affect how well we can draw inferences from it in order to modify and improve the unit.

In the Preface we suggested that, as a minimum level of activity, you go in with

(i) some ideas about what you hope will happen, emphasizing pupil and teacher activities
(ii) some questions that you want answered about the unit, and
(iii) some paper to note what actually does happen in detail, and in general.

Taking each of these suggestions in turn, we will try to offer possibilities that range from this simple scheme to a much more detailed and sophisticated level of observation. We shall offer a set of 'observation kits' at different levels of detail which offer a practical way of collecting information on what happens in the classroom. We begin by summarizing their elements before describing each of these. Again we are prescriptive, and you are free to choose or not.

Elements of observation kits

The fine observation kit
The observer will find that each of the following elements provides important and useful information:

(a) a short discussion with the teacher on class background and lesson intention, referring to the background checklist 7 (page 48)
(b) specific list of expectations and questions
(c) preview of printed material and other pupil resources to be used
(d) SCAN of substantial lesson segments taking in the range of activities which occur (see page 51)
(e) record of the affective interactions early and late in the lesson using the attitude checklist 8 (page 55)

(f) brief discussions with individual pupils to elucidate their responses to specific teaching points

(g) collection of selected pupil work for copying and return (if the teacher is willing, you may prefer to supply and collect the paper they work on)

(h) post-interview with the teacher to obtain his view of the lesson outcomes, including particular incidents and pupils — possibly leading on to discussion of the SCAN record and possible inferences from it about the material

(i) the teacher-report form left for filling in later.

At the end of the lesson, the observer will try to answer the prepared questions relating to the unit (b).

Coarse observation kit
This is a simplified version of the above with the event-by-event SCAN analysis replaced by a mini-SCAN record using the episode and activity checklists 6E and 6A.

The interview elements (a), (f) and (h) may also be more restricted, but should include those elements specified in the designer's questions.

No observation kit
This involves no outside observer but simply asks the teacher to fill in the teacher's report form (i) above. This form of 'observation' has very severe limitations not only because the teacher has a principal role in the lesson but because that role is likely to demand almost the whole of the teacher's attention, particularly at the most important moments.

Fine observation kit
We now return to each item in the fine observation kit.

(a) Discussion with the teacher
If you are going to the school yourself, you can probably collect quite a lot of this general information by chatting with the teacher and pupils and noting down details of the surroundings. The list will thus serve to jog your memory and ensure that you do not overlook significant items. If, however, a colleague has offered to go along and watch the lesson for you, it may well help if you underline the type of general information you would like back in addition to the notes on the lesson.

Background information checklist: Mark the questions you want to use. You should be interested in the following.

1. The *teacher's expectations* of the lesson, ie, what he hopes the pupils will do, achieve, etc.
2. The *designer's expectations* of the lesson (if it is not you).

You may also be interested in the following:

3. Pupil's background, ability, age, previous knowledge, etc.
4. How familiar the class or individuals in the class, are with the microcomputer.
5. Whether the program will be used more than once with this class.
6. Whether the class moved to a special room in order to use the computer.
7. Whether the pupils would normally meet the topic that the teaching unit supports.
8. What preparations were made for the lesson.
9. Whether specific plans to follow up the lesson have been made.
10. Whether the teacher regularly uses the microcomputer in his classroom.
11. Whether the teacher feels that this particular lesson was enhanced by the use of a computer program.
12. The mode of classroom activity, ie, why the class is working in groups, or together, or as individuals.
13. Whether the documentation with the teaching unit seems satisfactory.
14. Whether the teaching unit has been used with other classes — if so, whether the experience changed the teacher's approach to its use.
15. How long it took the teacher to become familiar with the control of the program and to consider how to use it with his pupils.
16. Whether the teacher felt under pressure from the material — either in time or level of demand.
17. How nervous the teacher feels about using this teaching unit.
18. How often the teacher uses audio-visual aids in his classroom.
19. What resources the teacher usually uses.
20. What the teacher's normal style of teaching is like.
21. How large the class is.

(b) Expectations and questions
We take the STORYLINE program EUREKA as an example. Some of the designer's ideas about what would happen and what pupil and teacher activities might occur were:

(i) children and teachers would be amused by the screen presentation
(ii) that the screen might dominate the situation

(iii) that teachers would possibly be engaged in a new activity
(iv) it could be used across a range of teachers and children
(v) children would be busy drawing graphs themselves
(vi) discussion on the interpretation of the graphs would be instigated.

With these and other predictions in mind, and with reference to the relevant checklists, the following list of questions was selected for initial classroom observation.

1. Initial draft
1. How did the unit fit with the time available?
2. Did it produce a lot of the intended pupil activity?
3. Did the teacher receive plenty of information about pupils' thoughts?
4. Is the program easy to drive?
5. Did the screen animation dominate the lesson?

2.1. Computer talents
1. Is the current speed adequate in the classroom?
2. Is the graph produced accurately enough or does it cause confusion?
3. Did the pictures motivate the children?
4. Is the high-resolution graphical display essential?
5. Is any of the animation unproductive, or over-elaborate?
6. Would sound effects help?
7. Is the time of computer responses adequately controlled at each point?

2.2. Program personality
8. Is the image presented attractive with a balance of vitality and strength?
9. Are the humourous touches universal and repeatable?

3. Teaching checklist
1. Was it suitable for the age and ability ranges of pupils?
2. Will it appeal to some teaching styles more than others?
3. Did the program contribute to the teacher's own development?

4. Drive system checklist
1. Are the options clear at each stage for the teacher?

(c) Preview of printed material and other pupils resources to be used
Factual information of a variety of kinds is relatively easily collected. It will include, for example, details of the section of the textbook or other

printed material involved in the lesson and any notes the teacher may have made as part of the lesson plan or as a record of events in the lesson. We may also collect factual information on the ability and attitude of individual pupils and on their background in the subject concerned; this last is of importance because the level of demand on pupils can only be judged in the knowledge of how far the material concerned is new to them and of their record of success or failure with it in the past.

(d) The classroom observation − intellectual transactions
We have now considered the general background information to the trial and also the specific points about the unit that we wish to check. That leaves item (iii) from the Preface − go in with some paper and note down what does happen. This brings us to the major problems of class observation. There will, of course, be much more information available than you can possibly record. Notes on a lesson are often of a vague and impressionistic kind, which makes it almost impossible to draw the kind of inferences needed for our purposes, while those particular instances that are recorded are often atypical, having caught the observer's attention for that very reason. There appears to be a need therefore for a structured framework of observation which concentrates the attention on the most important aspects of the interaction in the classroom from the point of view of the designer of the teaching material and of its use by the teacher.

It is because observers vary in their skill and experience that we have devised two related 'observation kits' which work at different levels of detail. The more detailed *fine observation kit* uses the SCAN (Systematic Classroom Analysis Notation) system (see reference 2) to give a detailed picture of the rhythm of the teaching dialogue with an emphasis on describing the levels of demand on the pupil and of guidance by the teacher. For observers who find the pace of the SCAN analysis too demanding, or who wish to concentrate on other things, the *coarse observation kit* uses checklists which the observer fills in at the end of each short teaching episode. The questions in the checklist are related to the same concepts as in the full SCAN event-by-event analysis, but the pace is more relaxed (see 6A and 6E).

Details of the SCAN system are given in reference 2; and we recommend you at least to read this document. SCAN could be described as a possible shorthand notation for observers. It looks at a lesson as a sequence of natural units of teaching and learning.

The 'activity' is the name given to the longest unit, it relates to the mode in which the teacher and children are working at a particular point in the lesson. For example, the activity might be the teacher in

51

exposition to the whole class (E), or in exposition to a group of 10 pupils (E_{10}).

Alternatively, the class may be working in groups of three or four (W_4) with individuals in dialogue with the teacher (D). During a lesson the activity mode may stay the same throughout or it may change several times.

Each activity will be made up of several episodes. An 'episode' is the name given to the smallest complete unit of teaching — this could be the teacher's revision of the previous lesson's work (revision episode) or explaining a particular point to the class (explanation episode) or coaching an individual child on a problem he is working on (coaching episode), etc.

SCAN itself also records the sequence of individual 'events' — these are the single items which form an episode — questions and answers, explanations, instructions, etc.

The other key aspects of teaching that it is useful to record are the *level of demand* that is placed on the pupil(s) at each stage and the *amount of guidance* that the teacher provides. No matter how you record the happenings in a lesson, these are important variables. SCAN classifies them as follows.

Level of demand
α *Recall* of a single fact, or the carrying out of a single act
β *Exercise* — the carrying out of a sequence of acts under the pupil's own 'control' or constructive recall of related facts (eg, in making definitions)
γ *Extension* of the pupil's previous experience through investigation or discovery.

Level of guidance
1. *Close* — the pupil sees the choice as between only a few alternative possibilities.
2. *Moderate* — requires connection rather than mere selection.
3. *Open* — minimal guidance for the demand involved.

For most people learning to SCAN requires some training and practice. The episode and activity checklists 6E and 6A which follow may be found useful even by the inexperienced observer. The episode checklist is completed at the end of each episode, while the activity checklist is completed each time the activity changes.

6A. Activity checklist
An activity is a section of a lesson in which the teacher and pupil assume constant roles. The SCAN paper distinguishes

- exposition: to the whole class E_W; to groups of five or more E_n
- dialogue: teacher with groups of less than five D; (see page 98 for a summary of SCAN notation).

This checklist is to be used at each change of activity.

1. Did the teacher catch the pupils' interest?
2. How long did it take the pupils to join in the activity?
3. Was the momentum of the activity effectively maintained?
4. What proportion of pupils were involved early/middle/late?
5. Was the pupil activity listening/answering questions/writing/ drawing/discussing/other/as intended?
6. How much pupil initiative was displayed?
7. Was the conclusion of the activity clear?
8. Were the tasks well judged on demand/guidance?
9. Did the computer play an essential role?
10. Did it dominate excessively?
11. Did it make inessential demands on the teacher?
12. Did the teacher seem in command of the program?
13. Did the teacher seem in command of the material?

6E. Episode checklist
An episode is the smallest complete unit of teaching in a lesson — the teacher's revising of the previous lesson's work, or explaining an argument to the class, or coaching an individual child on a problem he is working on (the SCAN paper gives a fuller discussion). This checklist is to be used at the end of each episode.

1. What kind of episode was it (see page 98)?
2. What was the general demand level?
3. Was it well judged?
4. What was the response to questions (percentage)?
5. What was the guidance level?
6. Was it well judged?
7. What proportion of pupils seemed in touch?
8. What pupil activity was manifest?
9. What proportion was so involved?
10. Was there any γ-level demand?
11. Was there any immediate response to it? (Note: if returned to later.)
12. How many pupils involved?
13. In what ways could adjusting the material or its use here have helped this episode (both corrections and ideas are useful)?
(The golden rule for recording: get it down, even if you miss the next nugget.)

With more experience the observer will find it worth learning to use the full SCAN system, since the event-by-event analysis shows very clearly the rhythm of the teacher's style and how the teaching unit and the program support or upset it. Try your own variant.

(e) The classroom observation — affective interactions
Pupil attitudes are also important. So far we have been concerned with the nature and effect of intellectual transactions in the classroom. While it is in these that we are primarily interested in for the development of teaching material, they are likely to be dependent on the climate of attitudes that prevails in the lesson. Methods exist for recording information about the affective domain; we believe that observations must include information of this kind.

The affective responses of pupils consist of those behaviours which indicate their attitudes and ultimately the values they hold. In this case their attitudes to the learning tasks in which teachers attempt to engage them, particularly work with computers, are the objects of inquiry. These may be analysed in various ways. One well-known list and classification of affective behaviours by Krathwohl *et al* (see reference 11) includes:

I. Receiving (attending)
− awareness
− willingness to receive
− controlled or selected attention
II. Responding
− acquiescence in responding
− willingness to respond
− satisfaction in response
III. Valuing
− acceptance of a value
− preference for a value
− commitment
IV. Organization
− conceptualization of a value, organization of a value system
V. Characterization by a value.

We shall here confine ourselves to level II since responding seems the only important category which can be assessed reasonably reliably by detached observation in real-time − the other categories all involve 'invisible' mental processes which can only be probed by substantial intervention through pupil interviews or testing. However, this limitation is not as serious as it may seem at first sight, since the thoughtful response may well be regarded as an adequate objective.

Therefore the following attitude checklist 8 is offered as one way of recording the responsive attitudes. Further notes on some of the questions are given after the list.

8. Attitude checklist
Before recording any detailed information on the lesson, it is important to ensure that the classroom atmosphere is such that the material and the teaching it supports are getting reasonable attention from the class. It is equally worth noting if the class is so tightly controlled as to inhibit seriously pupil response.

If the answer to any of the questions 1 – 4 is 'no', any other information collected should be disregarded as evidence on the material being developed.

1. Is the atmosphere in the classroom such as to allow attention to be paid to the tasks in hand?
2. Does the class recognize the tasks allotted?
3. Is the class working on these tasks to a significant extent?
4. Is the control over pupil activity sufficiently relaxed to allow significant pupil response?

The following questions relate to attitude to the tasks themselves.

5. Is the pupil under observation engaged in a learning task specifically (a) initiated by the computer, or (b) allotted by the teacher?
6. Is the pupil engaged in task-related behaviour additional to the specific instructions given (directly or indirectly) (a) by the computer, (b) by the teacher?
7. Given a choice of learning experiences, do pupils:

(a) choose computer-assisted learning (i) in general, (ii) in work with this particular unit (volunteering)?
(b) show willingness to continue computer-assisted learning when a change of activity is called for, eg, when bell goes for break (persisting)?
(c) show willingness to engage other pupils in task-related talk (publicizing)?
(d) use words in relation to the task which indicate satisfaction, eg, 'I've got it', 'great', 'fab', 'neat', 'interesting' (enthusing)?
8. What is the ratio of task-related activity to non-task-related activity?

Notes on questions 5 – 8. Question 5 relates to *acquiescence in responding.* This sub-category like the others in this class includes species of 'doing something about the phenomenon besides merely perceiving it'. At this the lowest level, what is done is done in a *compliant* way. In the case of computer-assisted learning, pupils who engaged in tasks only when directed to do so by their teacher and limited their responses only to those specifically indicated by the teacher would be functioning at this level. This may provide the first observable category of classroom behaviour for a workable schedule.

The next category beyond acquiescence (revealed in answer to Question 6) is a *willingness to respond,* which is characterized by pupils entering *voluntarily* into task-related behaviours to which they have not been specifically directed. Such a class of behaviours includes going on to another task of a kind similar to that assigned by the teacher at one level and exploratory behaviour at a 'higher' level. The pupil is not merely acquiescing but willingly entering into alternative task-related endeavours. Given that the observer is aware of the tasks set by the teacher this too should be readily observable category.

Finally in this responding category is the sub-set *satisfaction in response* (shown in answer to questions 7 and 8). The difficulty of applying this 'highest' of the three sub-categories of responding lies in the word 'satisfaction'. How can we know that a pupil derives satisfaction from (in this case) the learning tasks in which he/she is engaged? Directly or indirectly we could 'ask' him/her, but our requirement is that an observer acting at a distance can observe what a pupil *does* and thence *infer satisfaction in response.*

Given these or similar categories of observable behaviours, it is now necessary to decide *who* should be observed, *how often, for how long* and *under what circumstances?*

It is not feasible to observe all the pupils in a class of 30, so a sample must be taken for observation. We suggest that six is about as many as an observer can cope with. These six should ideally be selected at random from an alphabetical class list. The observer must ensure that the six named in the sample can be identified. (If this poses a problem the teacher may give every member of the class a coloured stick-on badge, one of five colours, with six pupils per colour, and all the observed sample having the same colour.) The time samples could be of one minute's duration, arranged so that each of the six pupils is observed in a regular cyclical sequence for parts of a teaching period. Thus, in a lesson lasting an hour, each pupil will have been observed for a maximum of 10 minutes spread at regular intervals over the hour. Four such one-minute episodes would often be enough. We suppose that in a typical case only part of a lesson will involve the computer. At other times or in other lessons non-computer-assisted learning will take place. This is an important advantage because potentially it allows the pupils affective response to two or more different types of learning tasks to be recorded. Each period of observation or each sequence of periods of observation, possibly on different days (or over a longer period) will provide a longitudinal 'case' study of six pupils' affective responses to computer-assisted learning and non-computer-assisted learning. This suggested method of observation has two other advantages. Potentially it can accommodate variations in pupils' affective responses and can enable the observer to differentiate between 'Hawthorne' effects and more permanent phenomena.

It is not in any way necessary to record the whole of the lesson from either the intellectual or the affective point of view; experience shows that it is possible to pick out segments of the lesson for detailed observation of either kind, which provide enough information for developmental purposes.

(g) Discussions with pupils and collections of pupils' work
Some individual pupil outcomes should also be recorded. Where written pupil work is produced, it obviously contains a great deal of information; something can be learnt about the general stage of understanding of the class by looking through such work after the lesson, while more is revealed if it is possible to discuss it with the pupil concerned. Post-interviews with the individual pupils should take place either a short time after the end of the teaching episode, or (less favourably) at the end of the lesson.

(h) Post-interview with the teacher
Talking to the teacher after the lesson is usually informative. Most of us have a certain elation after a successful 'performance' which relaxes inhibition and stimulates perception. Apart from getting the teacher's overview of what happened, how it related to what he had planned, and how he regarded the unit's contribution to events, the observer can often learn more about individual episodes. (The SCAN record is a big help here, providing a framework for detailed discussions.) You may find that you have misinterpreted some events because of lack of background information about the child concerned.

(i) Teacher report form
The enclosed example of a report form shows how helpful a few relevant comments from the teacher can be.

PROGRAM NAME	EUREKA / ISLAND

Notes on class, age
ability, background, etc

5th form low ability set – several of whom are quite rowdy & disenchanted with school.

Problems of
program use

Brief informal
report.
How much pupil activity?
Did it help some
specific concept?
Pupil material?
Will you use it again?

Began with Eureka for entertainment value – rather than Airtemp. Played with commands and then tried graph sketching. They had the general idea but soon lost interest. We tried Island – again enjoyment of use of computer – drawing islands, eh – but graphs a bit too difficult & not entertaining enough. Then we tried Pirates – this they really enjoyed – just the simple idea, coordinates 0–4, cold/warm clues.

Changes needed

Suggested uses and
possible age range

So, the graph programs were not very appropriate as teachers of the concepts – could be perhaps with more background – but quite good as an introduction to the computer & what it can do.

Any other comments

A better lesson than some with this class, less tension, eh, but programs not really appropriate level conceptually.

Any other dates for
trial where observers
would be welcome
Suggestions for other
(related) units

J. Godwood.

13 . 2 . 87

58

4. Planning your observation

When collecting figures for any statistical analysis it is clearly very important that the way in which the data is collected is planned with the analysis in mind. In the same way, the collection of information from the classroom from which we hope to draw inferences about teaching material must be such that distorting factors due to the circumstances of collection do not invalidate its use. Let us consider possible distortions and ways in which we can minimize their effect.

First of all, there seem to be several quite different types of trial dependent on the experience of the teacher in various respects. We classify this in the following way.

C = teacher with experience of teaching with a computer.
C̸ = teacher not experienced in using the computer.
D = teacher who has been involved in the design of the unit.
D̸ = teacher not involved in the design of the unit.
L = teacher who has taught lots of lessons with the unit.
L̸ = teacher about to teach his first lesson with the unit.

Now let us look at the possible combinations.

CD trials, for example, are no real test of the driving system and will mainly be useful in making decisions about the effectiveness of the unit in meeting the intentions of the designer. It is useful for these trials to cover quite a wide range of classes to test the reaction of different groups of children and also to give the teacher and observers the opportunity to see how effective their use of the unit becomes with experience. We suggest that you always differentiate between the educational effectiveness with a *new user* of the unit CDL̸, and the educational effectiveness after several lessons with it CDL.

L trials are usually more difficult to organize — the teacher may have to plan some considerable way ahead before you can observe lessons where he has used the program several times before.

CD̸ trials give a good opportunity to see if the driving system stands up to a teacher who was not involved in the design of the unit and CD̸L̸ and CD̸L trials separately show its effectiveness on first acquaintance and its effectiveness after the teacher is acclimatized to its use. They give the opportunity to judge whether the driving system is suitable for the new user, and whether it is irritating and over-protective of the experienced user; conversely, one that suits the latter may floor the former. This is really an essential part of the trial and sometimes may even result in two different driving systems being offered; the problem may equally be solved by gradually opening up fuller access to the unit, in that way reconciling the two different kinds of need within a single driving system.

¢D trials — the unit is on trial with a teacher very familiar with the unit, but unfamiliar with computer systems: surprisingly this can occur quite frequently with subject teachers who have been closely involved in the design but who are as yet unfamiliar with computers. They give valuable feedback on likely problems for the mass of *¢Ø* teachers.

¢Ø trials, with teachers who are new both to the unit and to the computer system, are important at the present time because most teacher users will be in this category. It is suggested in the Preface that the other types of trial should precede *¢Ø* trials, as they will almost certainly lead to changes in the teaching unit, which will improve its chances of surviving in this taxing environment.

It is possible that special introductory units should be produced to get teachers out of the *¢* category (TESTDRIVE goes some way towards this), but at present the *¢Ø¢* teacher is a challenge that every unit must face.

However the trials are organized, it is important to identify what type of trial any information is from before drawing inferences on the basis of it. Also very important, if at all possible, is to have some idea of a teacher's normal mode of operation. This is best obtained by systematic observation of his or her teaching of normal lessons not involving a microcomputer. Other aspects of distortion need to be taken into account before finally trying to sort out what the information indicates.

1. Enthusiasm and the Hawthorne effect — the stimulant of something new and exciting produces extra enthusiasm and normally enhances effectiveness — 'all educational experiments succeed'.
2. Inconvenience — the trials are liable to require the teacher to distort his plans for the course in order to accommodate the new material when asked.
3. Observer distortion — the presence of the observer in the classroom can itself upset the usual rhythm of activities.

We suggest that, providing the teacher and observer are well aware of the distorting factors in the report-back system, the damaging effect on the inferences drawn from the report will be minimized. The suggested checklist of background information, 7, is an attempt to help the recognition of these factors.

A curriculum development group that is working with a well-established teacher network will gradually be able to reduce these distorting factors. Systematic planning towards trials by members of the network could prove very beneficial. Having now, as far as possible, taken account of distorting factors, how can the observer, teacher and curriculum designer assess the success of the teaching unit in terms of its educational effectiveness? This is a much more difficult task and is so dependent on each specific teaching unit that it is difficult to produce a generalized structure. Indeed, during the observation period of various teaching units using computer programs we have seen the units used on many occasions in a very different fashion to that envisaged by the development team responsible for their design. The teacher's report forms will give information which goes part of the way towards judging the educational value of the unit. The example given on page 58 gives quite concise comments that were certainly very helpful to the designer. However, the careful use of the observation kits described in Chapter 3 is the most powerful tool in assessing educational effectiveness.

The section concludes with a diary describing the initial stages of development of a program — the teacher concerned was on an intensive course on the design and development of such units, and this was her first effort. The program has only just reached the material development loop, but it is nonetheless quite useful to look at its progress and comment on the development so far.

Diary for TECDV

January   Idea programmed roughly and checked
with designer.

Fri 6th Feb   Rosemary suggested adding perspective
view.

Tues 17th Feb   Watched designer teach lesson
without a computer. Alan suggested
adding orthographic view.

Wed 4th March   Hugh & Rosemary saw progress.
No immediate suggestions.

Mon 9th March   Alan came up to M.J. and he
and Rosemary made the following
suggestions.

Alan's suggestions	Rosemary's suggestions
a) "Chop" put in sooner.	a) "edge" lines on elevation optional.
b) Automatic pause too short.	b) plan, elevation, etc should be features.
c) Add 3rd type of perspective.	c) orientate shape.
d) Perspective same colour all over.	

(Before 20th March)   Facility to decide on order
of "features" added. Alan's
suggestions a, b, d & Rosemary's

62

c implemented & facility to give coordinates of vertices of plan to allow for R's ©.

Fri 20th March Group discussion – David suggested that the regular shape should be able to be rotated. John said that when user pressed a key, the result should always show. Austin wanted side elevation added.

Thurs 26th March First trial with 3rd form. Bug in program so that plan wouldn't show. Alan returned to blackboard – error quickly detected in time for successful run to follow. Obviously needed to be able to return to "plan". (Prog. allowed extra ?ing time for teacher.)

Fri 27th March Colin suggested all diagrams should be routed. Implementing this needed serious surgery which

Thurs 2nd April 2nd trial with parallel form. Driven successfully. Awaiting detailed report.

Fri 3rd April Group discussion. Facility to put in coordinates of "own shape" in any order requested.

Comments on the diary

Tuesday, 17 February — the designer observes the normal teaching mode of the teacher for whom the unit is, in the first instance, being prepared. This is not only good for comparison later but also adds another idea to the teaching unit for this class.

Monday, 9 March — the curriculum group now comments on a more advanced draft of the program — quite a few changes.

Friday, 20 March — more discussion with the experienced program design group. A month is spent in the design/development loop — the driving system changes considerably and extra features are added.

Thursday, 26 March — the first trial of the unit. A ~~C~~D~~L~~ trial with the teacher, who had been studied previously. The driving system needs to be more flexible. A new feature that allows the teacher to control the pace is successful.

Thursday, 2 April — moving towards ~~C~~DL or even CDL as the teacher learns to handle the system and the unit. The new driving structure seems successful.

Looking at the development so far, there is the need for CD trials in the near future; plans should also be made at this stage for ~~C~~~~D~~~~L~~ and ~~C~~~~D~~~~L~~ trials as they will take longer to organize.

5. Drawing inferences

The drawing of inferences from the information as it is obtained, like all such modes of thinking, is not susceptible to recipes. Skill in this will be an important factor in distinguishing good from mediocre curriculum designers. (In fact, we do not know how to do it, but it is important that you do it well!) The essence of the skill lies in diagnosing a mismatch between the designer's intentions and what happens in the classroom and then deciding if the mismatch is such that modifications in the unit are necessary. Sometimes the teacher uses a program quite differently from the way in which the designer has envisaged its being used. This does not necessarily mean that the program needs modifying — indeed it could be a positive sign that the unit can respond to a wide range of teaching styles.

Let us look at this in more detail. The observer detects a clear mismatch between the designer's intentions for pupil or teacher behaviour and what happened. He has recorded both, with a clear picture of the demand levels on the pupil at each stage and of the guidance provided by the teacher. If the teacher seemed quite happy with the episode involved, then in discussion after the lesson the observer can try to gather how the teacher feels about the intended pattern of behaviour, why it did not occur, and what can be done.

Possibilities	*Actions*
(a) The teacher did not recognize the possibility.	Improve documentation including:
(b) The teacher did not feel he could achieve it successfully.	more support in program or notes.
(c) The teacher preferred the alternative he chose.	Consider inclusion of this in the notes.
(d) The teacher was willingly diverted by the pupils.	As (c) and observe more lessons.
(e) The teacher was unwillingly diverted by the pupils.	More support and clearer guidance — (or dispose of pupils!)

Each of these suggests appropriate modifications to the unit — perhaps along the lines given in the right-hand column above. If the teacher is unhappy about the episode, or if the designer feels that it lay outside the realm of desirable behaviour, better protection of some sort is needed.

Once the observer decides that the mismatch of intended and actual activities is negative rather than positive as far as helping the children to learn is concerned, he will need to identify where modification is necessary. Referring to the checklists may well help; if serious problems are revealed, new ideas (see Chapter 2) may be needed.

We now take some actual examples of mismatch encountered during trials of units and discuss the inferences that might be, and were, drawn from them.

1. Teacher got confused in controlling the program to the extent that the lesson became disrupted. (This occurred in using JANE in a primary school in a ∅∅∠ trial.) In general we could surmise some possible causes:

− lack of clear guidance either in 'help routines' within the program or as printed instructions in the documentation accompanying the program
− lack of preparation, ie, reading the documentation, which may suggest the demands are too high for most teachers (teacher's guides are rarely read)
− poor 'driving system' within the actual program, ie, the central organization of the system does not match teachers' needs
− poor 'driving system' that either confuses the teacher through its complexity or, at the other extreme, is not flexible enough for him to achieve the flow of his planned lesson
− poor 'driving system' that interrupts the presentation of relevant displays with detailed control instructions on the screen.

In fact, in this case the unit was out on a ∅∅∠ trial with quite inadequate documentation − the only documentation we had at that time was such that we were frightened to show it to the teacher because we realized that it would 'finish him off'. This mismatch led to our including clear, key-by-key sequences in the notes and a resolution not to go out on ∅∅∠ trials before reaching the stage of adequate documentation, as time is too valuable. We should be prepared to test documentation at this stage.

In general, this type of problem indicates that some modification either to the program itself, or in the notes that communicate how to control it, will be needed. If, however, different teachers experience different problems of this nature and often fail to discover the full range of options that the program offers, it will indicate that the driving system of the program is too complex and obscure and most certainly needs modifying.

2. The teacher appears to fail to bring out an intended point in the unit. (An example occurred in a ∅∅∠ trial of TRANSPOTS.) In general

the causes could be:

- the teacher was inadequately aware of the point
- he concentrated on some other equally important point
- the documentation was either misleading or did not adequately stress the point
- the program presentation did not adequately support it.

In this particular case, we felt that the documentation did not adequately stress the point. The teaching unit was TRANSPOTS and the intended teaching strategy was that the children should be encouraged to develop their problem-solving skills by working in groups, to decide logically where best to place a factory to minimize transport costs. In the trial observed, the children tended simply to *guess* the factory location. Now it happens that everyone's instinctive belief that the best site is at the 'centre of gravity' of the sources and markets is incorrect in this problem — the best site tends to be at the source or at a dominant market in many cases: this point failed totally to emerge. In the lesson there did not seem to be any movement towards better understanding through exploring examples, as intended, or even towards using the guesses to encourage the type of investigative interactions the designer had envisaged. More guidance seemed necessary. Although the teacher may well have introduced this later, and indeed CDL trials did show evidence of this, we decided to include some carefully graded illustrations in the documentation that take the teacher through the type of discussion we would like to see the children taking part in.

In general, depending on the identified cause of such a mismatch, either the documentation of the unit will need modifying or the program presentation will need to emphasize the point more clearly. If the point is a really difficult one, it might be discretely abandoned.

3. The computer appears to dominate the whole scene to the detriment of constructive pupil activity (a common danger). In general, the cause could be:

- 'Hawthorne' effect of a new, highly motivating medium
- teacher relaxing too much into a supportive role to the computer
- too many different options offered by one program
- the game environment presented by the program too addictive.

TRANSPOTS as described above could provide the particular example again. However, another striking example of this type of mismatch arose when a student teacher C̸Ø̸L̸ used a very simple program that asked children to estimate angles: it was simple to run and at the time had no documentation. The children obviously enjoyed the activity, and it brought up some very interesting points about error in their estimation and other matters. The teacher did not take these up but remained 'glued' to the program as an activity. When asked why she allowed the computer so to dominate in this way, she replied 'It's the first time they have been quiet for a whole week!', reflecting the second cause in the list above. We decided that this could happen with quite a few units and that we should point out in the documentation the need to be on guard against it.

In general, the first cause, the Hawthorne effect, is not too serious, as it should wear off. The other three are more worrying. A good unit can be extremely supportive to the teacher but should not decrease the role that he alone can play best, ie, picking up and building on the pupils' reactions and suggestions. If this does appear to be happening there is a need either to warn the teachers in the unit documentation or maybe even to indicate possible dangers within the program.

Too many options within a single program tempt the teacher to try and use all of them in too short a period. A game environment may turn into a guessing sequence rather than a session that encourages logical reasoning, as illustrated in the example given above. If this tends to happen, very clear warnings need to be given in the unit documentation.

In order to start drawing useful inferences leading to sensible modifications of the material, we should also keep in mind these points:

(a) the observer must thoroughly understand the curriculum designer's aims and objectives and report in relation to these
(b) it is necessary for the observer to understand how the teacher has interpreted these intentions
(c) the curriculum designer must thoroughly understand the facts that the observer has brought back to him; the dialogue that this implies can produce valuable suggestions for improving the unit
(d) teachers of differing style must be observed and teachers at differing levels of acclimatization to the program must be observed to obtain full data
(e) it is also important for the observer to understand which stage of development the unit has reached.

Once changes have been made it is just as important to observe the modified unit in action as it was to conduct the initial trials.

It might help designers if a history of mismatches that arose during trials and the actions taken to correct them, was kept; indeed we feel that some of the particular cases do lead to useful generalization. Adopting a systematic approach to the analysis of the mismatches will help considerably in identifying them in future trials and deciding upon appropriate action.

6. Getting it used – dissemination and 'take-up'

Take-up

We tend naturally to concentrate on effectiveness – everybody does despite the evidence from curriculum development projects in all subjects that take-up is a far greater problem. (Unfortunately, the fact that many projects have produced attractive material which is extremely effective in the hands of *some* teachers but that has not been widely successful may reasonably be interpreted either as an aim- or a style-mismatch, or as a dissemination problem.) Let us, therefore, start with take-up and the stark reality of repeated Russian-roulette it contains. An alternative analogy may be more helpful. If 64 horses start a race of six fences and half of those left fall at each fence, how many finish? The hurdles in the dissemination race are:

H_0 – 'seeing' – saw advertisement
H_1 – 'getting' – obtained material
H_2 – 'browsing' – learned to drive the program
H_3 – 'trying' – used it once in the classroom
H_4 – 'using' – used it regularly in the classroom
H_5 – 'absorbing' – sustained use.

This too is a long sequence of fences at each of which interested but busy teachers will be 'lost'. The designer, aided by the development process must try to ensure that only a small proportion of teachers fall at each fence – a forbidding challenge.

In-service demonstrations in the schools of program units may avoid some of the perils of

H_0 – 'who reads publishers' advertisements?'
H_1 – 'who can be bothered, or afford, to order stuff?'
H_2 – 'I can't find time to work my way through that!'

This can work well with an enthusiastic teacher, or adviser, who can find the energy to organize the necessary demonstrations and workshops; it allows the teacher to enter the race with only three fences to go. It is however, expensive in time and effort. Team-teaching alongside a knowledgeable and enthusiastic colleague can effectively take one to the next stage. These are important factors in the superior success rates achieved by such methods of dissemination and in-service professional development.

How can we learn more of where the dissemination problems lie? Each step needs looking at differently. The first two hurdles H_0 and H_1, although separately observable, are closely linked since different advertising channels have different success rates — the leaflet to school may be easy to arrange (no falls at hurdle H_0) but is not very effective (all down at H_1), while word of mouth recommendations tend to have the reverse problems. In these early days of computer-based teaching units when there is very little effective material available, it is likely that any school with a computer will try to collect such material but then it will not necessarily reach all the relevant subject teachers; the chance of getting to H_2 and browsing through the program will then depend on communications within the school.

Getting over H_2 is very much our concern, and trials to ensure that teachers learning to 'drive the unit' have a low failure rate are essential, and quite possible. A short trial with JANE conducted by Richard Phillips in Nottingham, using volunteer PGCE students, found a very high success rate. Each student found out how to use all the facilities of the program from the documentation, including the drivechart, and then gave a short lesson to his peers. However, more time ($\simeq$ 1 hour) was required than might be regarded as desirable.

H_3 is hard to study under trial conditions since any school agreeing to help with trials is making some commitment to look at the materials beyond the norm. In principle, the reponse of less-involved teachers in the same school provides useful information and 'driving lessons' for all, followed by a wait-and-see approach to the use of the unit, provide valuable feedback.

The numbers getting over the last two hurdles can probably be found by a later survey, but the time involved is such that this will surely be a separate activity. It may well be worth surveying the teachers' *intentions* and, later, their *further use* as a guide to improving long-term take-up.

Publishing

A major problem is to organize the publication and dissemination of the educational software that has been designed across the country. This is happening in an extremely *ad hoc* fashion at present. Here we give a very preliminary discussion.

We have in this paper so far been much concerned with the systematic classroom development of teaching units, looking towards the publication of such units to a very wide audience. There are, however, different levels of publication that could be developed which would eventually help more material to become available at the professional level that we have been discussing.

Draft programs

Many schools that have microcomputers are already using programs that aid their own teaching. Mainly it will be the mathematics, science or computer studies teachers or the keen sixth-formers who are intrigued or stimulated to write such software. We often visit schools that are involved in testing teaching units to discover that overnight a new program has been written by a teacher to use in his afternoon lesson. Extremely good ideas may have been incorporated and in the hands of the teacher involved the program may prove a powerful teaching aid. However, very seldom does the program have any documentation or a comprehensible system of control. Even the programmer himself has difficulty in driving it two days later! At this level of production the program is useful only to its creator and cannot be disseminated further. In order to realize the potential of the large amount of software of this nature, we need a system of 'minimum documentation' that would allow this material to reach a wider audience. We suggest that the minimum target audience would be teachers in the same neighbourhood in schools with exactly the same computer system and available software utilities. To reach such a target audience we probably need, at the minimum,

(a) about two pages of description by the authors of each unit, telling the user how to load the program, how to drive it, and its limitations both educationally and technically — this information could be included on the disc or tape that loads the program
(b) some incentive to the programmer to document the program to this level, perhaps through its resulting acceptance into a 'library'
(c) assurance from those receiving the program that they will be prepared to deal with the problems that such draft programs impose — this implies that they must be fairly competent users of their computer system: they could not expect to get software support from the author, who is likely to be another teacher whose time is fully occupied
(d) some financial and organizational support for the distribution of programs, even if only on a cooperative basis
(e) that users of such programs should undertake to report to the authors (and to the library?) on the usefulness of each program received, and if they wish, to make recommendations for improvement.

Wider distribution

If national coordinators were able to liaise with regional coordination the fruits of this 'low-level' educational development could possibly be quite considerable. Any program that receives favourable reviews from enough teachers should be considered for

- distribution as it stands but on a national basis
- production to a professional standard
- transferability to other microcomputers
- publication by national system
- publication by commercial publishers.

The standard to which the work would have to be developed to be attractive to a commercial publisher involves a great deal of further work. The classroom development suggested in this paper assumes that to reach such a stage the finished unit would need to have the following.

1. Good documentation which would include

(a) a general introduction to the topic or concept that the teaching unit is concerned with and a brief description of its potential
(b) very clear instructions on how to drive the program, usually including a key-by-key sequence to introduce the user to it and a clear description of the full range of possibilities that it offers
(c) a description of some of the ways teachers have used the unit
(d) discussion of its educational objectives and suggestions for further use
(e) references to educational material that would provide support for this topic or concept
(f) a full annotated program listing with specifications of the different computer systems that would support the software.

2. A computer program developed to a professional standard including:

(a) good 'help' facilities
(b) a clear flexible driving or command system
(c) well-structured code
(d) ease of transferability; above all
(e) it should be very robust and protect users from thoughtless input errors.

Many other items could be added to this list; reference 10 gives details of a number of considerations that the programmer needs to keep in mind.

3. A machine-readable form available for the computer systems under 1f, ie, on cassette-tapes or discs.

4. A software support system to back it up provided by the publishing house.

We suggest that curriculum development groups should not be responsible for the distribution and support of software at this level. Their efforts at this stage should be channelled to the creative work they alone can tackle. If they meet the requirements of the above list, the dissemination and support of their material should be made possible by others with sufficient expertise to cope with it.

Any curriculum group that is involved in producing curriculum material for full publication on a national basis, or with commercial publishers, will need to become experienced not only with the creative part of the work but also with the administrative problems entailed. Time will be spent on planning the progress of the material and on liaising with the publishing house. Those already familiar with these tasks for normal teaching materials will need to allow considerably more time for liaison when the work includes computer-based materials. Publishers are only now becoming aware of many of the new problems that producing and distributing computer programs will present, and publication methods for such material must be considered experimental at this stage. We advise groups or individuals that are producing work for publication to consult with others engaged in the same activity. As mentioned earlier, the art of editing material is one that has to be acquired; it is time-consuming and any group able to acquire the talents of an experienced editor will be well advised to do so.

On teacher development

We shall now expound a somewhat deeper theoretical model of the processes the teacher must go through in absorbing innovations, particularly those involving changes of teaching style, into their day-to-day teaching practice. We hope it will help to illuminate the problems the designer faces in trying to promote such changes by introducing new material.

One way of regarding the problem of disseminating innovative teaching practices is to assume that teachers have some kind of mental picture of the paths taken by their pupils' developing minds as they move through a topic (topic X) towards a state which may be thought of as 'understanding X'. X is usually identified by its subject matter, but any claim to understand X usually requires the demonstration of skills through the carrying out of specific tasks, in the form of exercises or problems, that relate to X.

The repertoire of transactions in which teachers engage their pupils when teaching X depends, among other things, on the nature of X and on the mental picture of the pupils' developmental path held by the teacher; the teaching will presumably be, in the teacher's eyes, consistent with these factors and at some levels, demonstratively effective. Innovations in teaching methods do not usually come in the form of simple additions to a teacher's repertoire, generalizable to all subject matters, but are usually designed to achieve more effectively an understanding of some particular X. Usually, for a variety of reasons, the descriptions of 'how to proceed' are not at a level of precision which makes the teacher a programmed automaton; it follows that any teacher persuaded to adopt the innovation must be willing and able to explore modifications to his repertoire in order to try and achieve the hoped-for improvement in his pupils' understanding of X at which the innovation is aimed.

This situation poses at least two kinds of threat to the teacher. First, the new approach may make the teacher aware of some lack of understanding of X — the originator of the innovation may well have a more comprehensive understanding of the topic and possibly a more detailed map of children's paths towards it but neither is in fact essential for the promotion of the feeling of insecurity in the teacher. Secondly, the demands made by the innovation on the teacher's repertoire of transactions may be greater than that which the teacher is accustomed to, or in the context of the particular class, is willing to risk trying.

It is, of course, more than likely that the teacher has no clear idea of the new elements of teaching involved, particularly if these involve extending his range of style; printed material in particular seems to be a largely ineffective way of communicating such information.

The use of an interactive computer as an aid to teaching involves programs, each of which has an identifiable range of content or subject matter X, the program provides a preset repertoire of computer 'comments' and 'responses' from which the teacher can select particular elements using the driving system; these are designed to promote transactions with the pupils and the teacher aims at moving towards 'understanding X'. These may or may not lie outside the range of transactions which the teacher may ordinarily use, but in order to exploit the system to the full for the purpose for which it was designed, it is necessary that the teacher using the system behaves in a way which is consistent with its purpose. For example, if a program calls for divergent responses to open questions and the teacher only accepts responses which he deems to be 'correct', then the potential of the program to stimulate divergent thinking will be at least partly thwarted. The result will be less effective than would be achieved by a teacher in harmony with the unit; indeed the contribution of the unit may have, on balance, been destructive. The power of the microcomputer, with its television screen, in affecting the classroom situation is such that it is less likely that a teacher can bend a unit away from its designer's intentions towards his own style and purpose than is the case with printed material.

These are the grounds for our repeated assertions that the designer of the unit must ensure that it only demands an achievable extension of the repertoire of transactions of the teachers for whom it is intended. Classroom development is the only way we know of ensuring that this condition has been met.

One may therefore think of an innovation in teaching methods as being designed to *achieve a set of intentions* (eg, changes in pupils' ways of thinking) by means of *a set of processes* which are usually only rather coarsely determined. The results of these processes will be a set of *outcomes,* hopefully but not always involving observed changes in the behaviours of the pupils. The successful trial of the system requires that the teachers understand and accept the intentions, and that they are able and willing to engage in the processes implied. Furthermore, it is important that, with assistance if necessary, they can observe the response of their pupils to these processes and see that their short- and medium-term effects are consistent with the intentions.

We believe that it is possible to describe the intentions in a comprehensible way. The microcomputer provides a powerful new way of stimulating and directing teaching and learning processes. We may need to devote more attention to helping the teacher discern their effects and to relate them to the intentions.

7. Has classroom development helped?

Evaluation

How can we judge how far the development system we are advocating, or any other, meets our expectations? We want to evaluate it. As usual the aims of this can be formative (to improve it) or summative (is it worth using?). We shall take a down-to-earth approach which avoids the fallacy that only quantitative information is of value, while accepting the power of valid measures.

Impressionistic data

We begin with impressionistic data, proceeding later to suggest more systematic approaches. 'It' refers to the development system.

(a) Look at it. The design of the system merits due examination to see how far each of its elements serves its aims – both in theory and in practice. The various facets will surely have been argued over intensively and extensively but it may be worth looking at what each objective is supposed to contribute and how far it has done so.

(b) Does it get used? It is then worth examining informally what happens in practice – whether the expected information seems to be acquired and how effective the inferences drawn from it are in relation to the cost. This approach will extend to more systematic studies.

(c) Does it feel right? It is an important, though not overriding, aim that the system should appeal to those who use it, feeling naturally supportive to the user and effective in the class. Attitude studies can be made and changes made to ease problems they reveal.

(d) Does it lead to action? The aim of the system is to develop the unit so that it will be more effective in the classroom with more teachers. It is straightforward to record suggestions made by observers, and how far these are adopted.

It is equally clear that there is a need for some element of experimental control in the evaluation exercise, if the results are to have more force than an expression of informed opinion. This leads to more systematic possibilities of which there are a number. We shall note two as illustrations.

Sequential evaluation of the system
This approach challenges the development system to make significant cost-effective improvements in a unit which has already been substantially developed without much classroom observation. JANE was processed rather along these lines. The method is (1) develop the unit informally, then 'freeze' it to give version 1, and (2) then put it through development machinery such as that suggested in this paper, to give version 2. We then compare versions 1 and 2. There are at least two grounds for comparison.

(a) Are there any changes? What are they? Are they workable? Such questions are fairly easy to answer, and the answers will give rise to a subjective impression on the designer's part as to whether the unit has been improved, and whether it was worth the effort.

(b) Compare the effectiveness of version 1 and version 2. Here we would wish to emphasize measures based on CØ£ and CØL users, unless the unit is specifically designed to introduce people to computers as a teaching aid. We can

− compare the attitude of teachers to the two versions
− watch each in action, and form judgements on their effectiveness based both on the positive transactions in the lessons and on the problems that the unit causes
− compare their effectiveness in helping pupils learn the topic or concept involved − this is difficult, since the unit is likely only to be a small part of the pupils' educational experience.

Parallel evaluation of the system
In this approach, the draft program is developed in parallel by two separate groups. (1) Version 1 is developed informally by a group of believers in this approach. (2) Version 2 uses a systematic classroom development method.

The comparison of the two versions will again note the differences between the two programs, though now it may be less easy to decide, even subjectively, whether changes are or are not improvements. Comparisons of their effectiveness can follow the same lines as in the sequential method above.

At this early stage of exploration of possibilities for classroom development we do not believe that it is possible conclusively to decide on their effectiveness. None the less, as with any suggested procedure, we think it important to have in mind ways of deciding whether or not they succeed or fail.

Appendix A. Programs

PIRATES[1]

The PIRATES program is a treasure hunt in a two- or three-dimensional grid. The treasure is found by a process of successive guesses. Following each attempt the computer responds with some helpful information. The nature of the clues varies. You may choose from:

1. Compass directions
2. Simple 'getting warmer/colder' messages
3. Bearing and elevation responses
4. Clues in the form of vectors
5. Distance clues

Many different strategies emerge in the various 'games' and a great deal of mathematical activity is promoted in the classroom. It is suitable for a wide range of ages (8 – 18 years) and abilities, as the teacher is responsible for setting the level of demand.

·One teacher comments, 'This exercise found the pupils highly motivated and eager to succeed. You rarely see pupils so eager to get questions right.'

The package contains:

Teacher's handbook – PIRATES
Computer program – PIRATES (PIRA)
Teacher's handbook – GUIDE TO THE USE OF DRIVECHARTS
Computer program – TESTDRIVE (TESTDR)

It is available in the first issue for 380Z and PET machines.

81

TRANSPOTS[5]

Although the program which supports this unit sets up an environment based on the south-west of England to consider the problem of locating a factory to manufacture goods using china clay as a major raw material, it is an example that can be used in both geography and mathematics lessons to promote a great deal of thought and discussion that are of general benefit. For the geography teacher it offers work on:

1. Defining positions on a map
2. Considering the costs of materials and transport
3. Problem-solving at different levels
4. Introduction to the idea of location theories

For the mathematics teacher it offers work on:

1. Plotting points on a graph
2. Arithmetic — especially ratios
3. Problem-solving at various levels
4. Introduction to problem-solving and logic

The age-range is 11 – 18 years in both subjects.

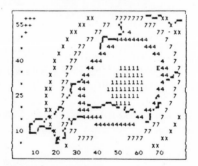

JANEPLUS[4]

This unit encourages children to discuss the idea of simple mathematical functions. It can be used across a wide age-range (5 – 18 years old) and also across a wide ability-range. It provides the teacher with the opportunity to pose questions in a motivating environment. Small figures of children appear on the screen and by observing how 'they' change numbers it is possible to discuss what 'they' might be doing. The program is extremely flexible and easy to control — it allows the teacher to set up a large variety of investigations.

FRED JULIE

STORYLINE

STORYLINE consists of three programs which aim to develop pupil skills in interpreting and sketching graphs of realistic situations, emphasizing a qualitative discussion of global features with no plotting or reading of individual points.

The Cartesian convention is explained, graphically of course, in AIRTEMP where a moving thermometer produces a graph of temperature variation with time.

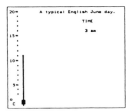 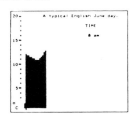 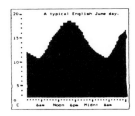

In EUREKA simple entries (T = taps on or off, etc) allow the construction of scenarios for taking a bath; the cartoon illustration of what occurs is matched by a graph of water-level against time, either of which can be suppressed if pupils are to sketch the curve or interpret the graph. A replay facility allows the results to be described and discussed.

 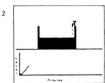

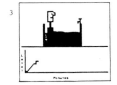 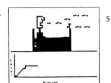

Finally ISLAND shows and plots the number of burned trees on an island (the shape can be controlled) against time. The program offers the user the facility to draw his 'own' island and also to superimpose graphics from various islands on the screen so that the different situations can be discussed and compared.

A high-resolution graphics display or a low-resolution graphics display are available as options in both EUREKA and ISLAND.

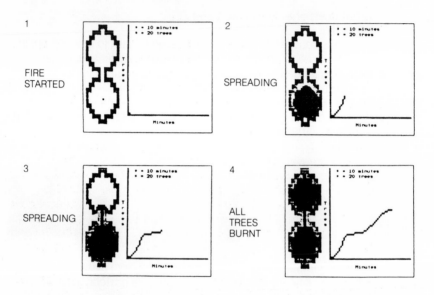

1   FIRE STARTED

2   SPREADING

3   SPREADING

4   ALL TREES BURNT

The STORYLINE collection has not yet been published but EUREKA is available, for example in reference 12 which includes 14 program teaching units.

Appendix B. Checklists and observation kits

Here we collect the various checklists provided in this paper and the observation kit described in Chapter 3; the full SCAN system as given in reference 2 is not reproduced here but the notation set is summarized at the end of this appendix.

1. Initial draft checklist (see page 20)
Notes
The first stage in the development of a unit is discussion between the people or groups representing curriculum development, program development and classroom use. The first questions on this checklist can be considered at the very early discussion of the idea and help to formulate the first draft computer program and the teachers' guidance notes which are the start of the unit's documentation. When considering each question you should be careful to think of the documentation and notes as well as the computer program.

In the same way, when predicting the type of lessons that may occur, remember the computer program, the documentation and the teacher all play roles in the success or failure of a session. It is important to consider which of these is in need of adjustment or how protection can be offered to try and avoid obvious pitfalls that could undermine the unit's effectiveness. If you wish the unit to be widely useful you should not expect a teacher's style to have to change significantly.

Once a rough draft of program and documentation is reached, we suggest four or five lessons are simulated with the close group of people working on the draft; deliberately try to explore the different lesson types that may be possible (see question 2 and Chapter 3). These mini-trials will be better than pure speculation and will enable you to tackle questions 15 – 23 with some preliminary evidence in front of you.

Initial draft checklist
This checklist is designed to be used during and after the initial drafting stage of the program and teaching material.
1. What is the unit trying to do (concepts, content, etc)?
2. What pattern of lesson activity is it envisaged to support (revision, introduction, etc, or expository, investigatory, small groups, whole class etc, or teacher-centred, pupil-centred, machine-centred)?
3. What pattern of pupil activity is envisaged? What level of demand and guidance might be appropriate?
4. What age/ability range is the target?

5. How much time does the unit need in the curriculum: one lesson, half a lesson, a whole term?
6. Does it tackle a recognized teaching problem?
7. Which bits of standard textbooks does it relate to?
8. Does any indicated approach in the program design set up hurdles for further conceptual development?
9. Can you write a brief report of four different lessons that you envisage could take place with this material?
10. What uses of the unit do you envisage could weaken its effectiveness? Can program or documentation protect the user?
11. What does the unit allow the teacher to try and do?
12. Is the scope of the unit too broad?
13. Is the freedom left for the teacher too narrow?
14. What computer talents seem likely to increase effectiveness?
15. Is the unit doing what you hoped for?
16. Is it effective in the time-span envisaged?
17. Does it produce a lot of the intended pupil activity?
18. Does the teacher receive plenty of information about pupils' thoughts?
19. Does the program seem to take on roles more suited to the teacher?
20. Are there aspects of support that are more suited for the program to provide?
21. Is the program easy to drive?
22. Are the decisions structured naturally?
23. Is there a danger of undesired dominance — machine, teacher or pupils?
24. How far does the program command pupils' attention?
25. Can you give the teacher a clear indication of when the microcomputer should be turned off?
26. What is the worst thing that could go wrong if someone makes a mistake using your program?

2.1. Computer talents (see page 22)
2.1s. Speed
1. Is the current speed adequate?
2. Will transfer to other common microcomputers cause speed problems?
3. Is the teacher still being asked to process things the computer could help with?
4. What related information could easily be provided? Does it really contribute?

5. Is the speed of presentation under enough teacher or program control? For example, if run with a different system or even a different interpretation in the same system, will it behave properly?

2.1g. Graphics
1. Do the screen images present all and only the information desired?
2. Does the image clearly focus attention on the essential elements without distraction?
3. Is the size and timing of images such as to make them easily visible to all the pupils?
4. Does the computer give information that might better come from the teacher or the pupils (consider each point in turn, linking it to the envisaged teacher and pupil activities)?
5. Do the images positively stimulate pupil discussion and pupil activities?
6. Is your use of high resolution or colour essential, or even productive?
7. Is the program written as far as possible in a way that will ease transferability?
8. Have you consulted a graphic designer about this unit?

2.1a. Animation
1. Is animation exploited to give vitality and variety to the images at the best points?
2. Are there concepts that could be better brought out by an animated sequence?
3. Is it used well in providing reward stimuli?
4. Could animation be used to add an extra dimension to the displayed information?
5. Is any of the animation unproductive or over-elaborate?

2.1e. Extended device control
1. Would audio output (bell, voice, etc) help the impact?
2. Would other display media contribute importantly — slides/film/video?
3. Has the unit essential conceptual links with apparatus?
4. Is this link clearly established for the pupils?
5. How can this be demonstrated?
6. Could the computer usefully be physically linked to the apparatus in question?

2.1i. Input and output devices
1. Has the flexibility of response to any input been explored to make operations simple?
2. Are there any potential benefits from the use of:
(a) mouse
(b) touch screen
(c) lightpen
(d) graphics pad
(e) voice input
(f) voice output
(g) special purpose devices?
3. In view of the loss of transferability, should these be optional?
4. Does their use compensate for any increased program complexity?

2.1t. Timing
1. Is the timing of computer responses adequately controlled at each point?
2. Is the time control left to the teacher appropriate?
3. Is the basic timing reasonably stable (eg, independent of system software changes) and transferable?

2.1r. Randomization
1. Has the possibility been explored for:
− computer generated examples
− random computer stimuli
− realism in simulation?

2.2. Program personality (see page 25)
1. Is the image presented attractive, with a balance of vitality and restraint?
2. Has this been informally tested?
3. Are the humorous touches universal and repeatable?
4. Have the possibilities for warmth of response been explored?
5. Do failure and success get effective, encouraging responses of criticism and praise?
6. Is eventual success for all the pupils built in?
7. Does the balance of patience and impatience generate momentum?
8. Is it adequately under the control of the teacher?
9. Is the rhythm of the program such as to produce the desired pattern of tension and relief?

2.3. Program style (see page 26)
1. Have the various style possibilities:
– neutral
– expository
– investigatory
– competitive
– cornucopian
– diagnostic
been systematically considered?
2. Is the maximum useful range of style opportunities provided?

3. Teaching checklist (see page 28)
1. Have you a clear view of how the teaching unit may be used by a variety of teachers?
2. How can you help the teacher to use the unit effectively?
3. Which of the following activities will the program help the teacher with:
(a) introducing a new topic
(b) exercises to help strengthen understanding
(c) progression through a topic
(d) revision of a topic or topics
(e) problem-solving activities?
4. What age and ability range of pupils is the material suitable for?
5. Will it appeal to some teaching styles rather than others?
6. Does the program try to assume ideas that would be best left to the teacher?
7. Can the program contribute to the teacher's education?
8. Can the program be used in more than one subject area?
9. Can the program be used to produce teaching material?
10. What concepts does the program tackle?
11. Does the program link different aspects of the curriculum together?
12. Does the program cater for different levels of presentation?
13. What type of flexibility does the program offer the teacher?
14. Does the program provide aids to memory (visual impact, mnemonic aids, etc), and if so, how?
15. What motivation does the program offer?

4. Drive system checklist (see page 35)
1. Are the program options logically structured in teaching terms?
2. Are the options at each stage clear for the teacher?
3. Are there any redundant key-strokes?
4. Is the global option structure clearly presented?
5. Does it indicate the full range of possibilities?

6. Are the help facilities clear, and easily called?
7. Is there any redundant information on the screen?
8. Is it likely that it will attract the attention of, and thus distract, children?
9. Have you planned to test the efficiency of the system with mathematical and non-mathematical teachers at all levels — experts, enthusiasts, volunteers and sceptics?
10. Could the range of facilities usefully be extended without producing an impenetrable driving system?
11. Can the program be operated with a useful limited subset of the facilities? Does the driving system make this clear?

5. Programming checklist (see page 39)
1. For which system or systems is the program being developed?
2. Are these systems available to schools now or in the near future?
3. Have you chosen a system because of peculiar non-transferable features? If so, would you consider modifying the requirements to make them more transferable?
4. Do you know details of the ROM monitor and operating system and what this implies?
5. Do you know the version of BASIC or another language to be used?
6. Do you know how much memory will be available for the program?
7. Is the suggested program likely to fit into this memory size?
8. What additional storage facilities are provided for the machine?
9. What additional hardware devices are provided for the system?
10. Are you fully aware of the facilities provided by the 'standard' machine?
11. Are you aware of the range of facilities which can be added through software routines in machine code?
12. Are you aware of additional facilities provided by hardware?
13. Do you know the overheads of using standard software, special software and hardware in terms of speed, memory use and transferability?
14. Have you established which facilities will be necessary for the successful implementation of the program?
15. Are they likely to produce a sufficiently good performance for the user?
16. Does the necessary set of facilities exist on a system which is practical for schools?
17. Is the speed of the program fast enough but not too fast?
18. Is the program logically crashproof?
19. Are all possible user errors trapped and help messages provided?

20. Are there any operations in the use of the program which would be at all complicated to a user inexperienced in the use of a computer system?

21. Is the internal structure of the program as efficient as it needs to be for good performance?

22. Which are the critical routines to optimize for speed and for memory size?

23. Is the program logically structured?

24. Is the program easily understood by the author — and by others?

25. Is there an available 'library' of subroutines which may help towards meeting the requirements of this program?

26. Are there any conventions for variables or routines agreed for this program unit to aid readability, set by yourself, your establishment, a national body or publishers?

27. Is the program adequately documented for the user to be able to feel at home with it from the start?

28. Is the program adequately documented for the author and other programmers or interested people to understand its operation clearly?

29. Are any 'special' routines documented in detail?

30. Is the program intended to be portable or transferable? If so have common characteristics been established as being practical? Are all machine-dependent routines written in clearly documented subroutines? Do the equivalent routines on the other systems perform adequately?

31. Have you discussed any possible areas of difficulty in implementation with the others in the design team, so that alternative approaches could be considered if necessary?

32. Are you sufficiently confident about being able sucessfully to complete a program which will perform well enough to meet the design specification, and which will thus justify spending a large amount of your time?

6A. Activity checklist (see page 52)

An activity is a section of a lesson in which the teacher and pupil assume constant roles. The SCAN paper distinguishes:

exposition — to the whole class E_W, or to groups of 5 or more E_n
dialogue — teacher with groups of less than 5 D
W_n — pupils working in groups of n.

This checklist is to be used at each change of activity.

1. Did the teacher catch the pupils' interest?

2. How long did it take the pupils to join in the activity?

91

3. Was the momentum of the activity effectively maintained?
4. What proportion of pupils were involved early/middle/late?
5. Was the pupil activity listening/answering questions/writing/drawing/discussing/other/as intended?
6. How much pupil initiative was displayed?
7. Was the conclusion of the activity clear?
8. Were the tasks well judged on demand/guidance?
9. Did the computer play an essential role?
10. Did it dominate excessively?
11. Did it make inessential demands on the teacher?
12. Did the teacher seem in command of the program?
13. Did the teacher seem in command of the material?

6E. Episode checklist (see page 53)
An episode is the smallest complete unit of teaching in a lesson — the teacher's revising of the previous lesson's work, or explaining an argument to the class, or coaching an individual child on a problem he is working on (the SCAN paper[2] gives a fuller discussion). This checklist is to be used at the end of each episode.

1. What kind of episode was it (see page 98)?
2. What was the general demand-level?
3. Was it well judged?
4. What was the response to questions (percentage)?
5. What was the guidance-level?
6. Was it well judged?
7. What proportion of pupils seemed in touch?
8. What pupil activity was manifest?
9. What proportion was so involved?
10. Was there any γ-level demand?
11. Was there any immediate response to it? (Note if returned to later.)
12. How many pupils were involved?
13. In what ways could adjusting the material or its use here have helped this episode (both corrections and ideas are useful)?
(The golden rule for recording: get it down, even if you miss the next nugget.)

7. Background information checklist (see page 48)
Mark the questions you want to use. You should be interested in the following.

1. The *teacher's expectations* of the lesson, ie, what he hopes the pupils will do, achieve, etc.
2. The *designer's expectations* of the lesson (if it is not you).

You may also be interested in the following.

3. Pupils' background, ability, age, previous knowledge, etc.
4. How familiar the class or individuals in the class, are with the microcomputer.
5. Whether the program will be used more than once with this class.
6. Whether the class moved to a special room in order to use the computer.
7. Whether the pupils would normally meet the topic that the teaching unit supports.
8. What preparations were made for the lesson.
9. Whether specific plans to follow up the lesson have been made.
10. Whether the teacher regularly uses the microcomputer in his classroom.
11. Whether the teacher feels that this particular lesson was enhanced by the use of a computer program.
12. The mode of classroom activity, ie, why is the class working in groups, or together, or as individuals?
13. Whether the documentation with the teaching unit seems satisfactory.
14. Whether the teaching unit has been used with other classes — if so, whether the experience changed the teacher's approach to its use.
15. How long it took the teacher to become familiar with the control of the program and to consider how to use it with his pupils.
16. Whether the teacher felt under pressure from the material — either in time or level of demand.
17. How nervous the teacher feels about using this teaching unit.
18. How often the teacher uses audio-visual aids in his classroom.
19. What resources the teacher usually uses.
20. What the teacher's normal style of teaching is like.
21. How large the class is.

8. Attitude checklist (see page 55)

Before recording any detailed information on the lesson, it is important to ensure that the classroom atmosphere is such that the material and the teaching it supports are getting reasonable attention from the class. It is equally worth noting if the class is so tightly controlled as to inhibit seriously pupil response.

If the answer to any of questions 1 — 4 is 'no', any other information collected should be disregarded as evidence on the material being developed.

1. Is the atmosphere in the classroom such as to allow attention to be paid to the tasks in hand?
2. Does the class recognize the tasks allotted?
3. Is the class working on these tasks to a significant extent?
4. Is the control over pupil activity sufficiently relaxed to allow significant pupil response?

The following questions relate to attitude to the tasks themselves.

5. Is the pupil under observation engaged in a learning task specifically (a) initiated by the computer, or (b) allotted by the teacher?
6. Is the pupil engaged in task related behaviour additional to the specific instructions given (directly or indirectly) (a) by the computer, (b) by the teacher?
7. Given a choice of learning experiences, do pupils
(a) choose computer assisted learning (i) in general, (ii) in work with this particular unit (volunteering)?
(b) show willingness to continue computer assisted learning when a change of activity is called for, eg, when bell goes for break (persisting)?
(c) show willingness to engage other pupils in task-related talk (publicizing)?
(d) use words in relation to the task which indicate satisfaction, eg, 'I've got it', 'great', 'fab', 'neat', 'interesting' (enthusing)?
8. What is the ratio of task-related activity to non-task-related activity?

Fine observation kit (see page 48ff)
The observer will find that each of the following elements provides important and useful information:

(a) a short discussion with the teacher on class background and lesson intention, referring to the background checklist, 7
(b) specific list of expectations and questions
(c) preview of printed material and other pupil resources to be used
(d) SCAN of substantial lesson segments taking in the range of activities which occur
(e) record of the affective interactions early and late in the lesson using the attitude checklist, 8
(f) brief discussions with individual pupils to elucidate their responses to specific teaching points
(g) collection of selected pupil work for copying and return (if the teacher is willing, you may prefer to supply and collect the paper they work on)

(h) post-interview with the teacher to obtain his view of the lesson outcomes, including particular incidents and pupils — possibly leading on to discussion of the SCAN record and possible inferences from it about the material
(i) the teacher-report form left for filling.

At the end of the lesson, the observer will try to answer the prepared questions relating to the unit (b).

Coarse observation kit

This is a simplified version of the above with the event-by-event SCAN analysis replaced by a mini-SCAN record using the episode and activity checklists, (6E and 6A).

The interview elements (a), (f) and (h) may also be more restricted, but should include those elements specified in the designer's questions.

No observation kit

This involves no outside observer but simply asks the teacher to fill in the teacher's report form (i) above. This form of 'observation' has very severe limitations not only because the teacher has a principal role in the lesson but because that role is likely to demand almost the whole of the teacher's attention, particularly at the most important moments.

Nine stages of development

Writing	*Development*
1. State aims, targets, intentions, etc.	Discuss with interested group, observe lessons if relevant — brainstorm ideas. Check idea against aims, targets, etc. Discuss intentions, use draft checklist I.
2. Ideas accepted — write down intentions and behaviour (see Chapter 2 of this paper and checklists 1, 2, 3 & 4).	Establish the group of interested developers — think ahead to classroom lessons. If possible watch teachers with their normal lessons and get to know the background.
3. Draft the program into code with some minimum notes on how to operate it and what you hope for in the classroom (see Chapter 2 and checklists 2 and 5).	Discuss the draft program with the group — discuss lessons that could be given. Try it out on as many people as possible. Make sure it is easy enough to control (see Chapter 2 and checklist 4).

4. Revision of draft program ready for first classroom trial.

Take the program into the classroom yourself, with others to observe if possible (see Chapter 3).

5. Write a report on the progress so far.

Decide whether to continue or abort at this stage.

6. More revision if necessary. In particular begin to make clear notes on the control of the program and start to map out teaching notes (see Chapter 6 and checklist 4). These will expand as you receive development experience.

Other teachers within the group try it out in the classroom — again where possible with observers or with yourself as observer (see Chapters 3 and 6 and checklists 3 and 4). You should prepare well for this stage (see Chapter 4).

7. Rewriting in view of the evidence. Give special consideration again to your stated intention, etc, revised in the light of experience (see Chapter 5 and checklists 1 and 3).

Continue to watch as many lessons as possible in order to get enough information for the final documentation. Try to include users who have used the unit several times, in particular to check that the driving system remains effective and does not become irritating with repetition (see Chapter 4).

8. The program must now be polished up to include enough 'user support', etc (see Chapter 5). Also the documentation must give as clear an indication as possible to the user of the teaching possibilities (see Chapter 6 and checklist 3).

More trials with a wider audience — check that the 'driving system' helps to educate users in the use of the teaching unit (see Chapter 6 and checklist 4) — also trials on the unit's documentation. The unit must be able to survive alone (see Chapter 6).

9. Final production of material suitable for publishing (see Chapter 6 and checklist 5).

Final material should now be circulated to teachers for final comments and editing (see Chapters 4 and 6).

References

1. ITMA teaching unit 'PIRATES', Longman Micro Software, 1982
2. *SCAN — Systematic Classroom Analysis Notation,* Beeby, T, Burkhardt, H, Fraser, R, Shell Centre for Mathematical Education, University of Nottingham, 1979
3. SRC/ITMA development program 'AUTOFRACTIONS', 1980
4. ITMA teaching unit 'JANEPLUS', Longman Micro Software, 1981
5. ITMA teaching unit 'TRANSPOTS', Longman Micro Software, 1982
6. *Science Teaching Observation Schedule,* Eggleston, J J, Galton, M J, Jones, M E, 'Process and Products of Science Teaching', Schools Council Resource Series, Macmillan, 1967
7. ITMA guide 'HOW DRIVECHARTS WORK', Longman, 1981
8. *The SMALLTALK — 76 Programming System: Design and Implementation,* Ingalls, D, Conference report of Annual ACM symposium on 'Principles of Programming Languages', Tucson, Arizona, 23 – 25 January, 1978
9. ITMA project paper, *Development of Computer-Based Material for Use in the Classroom,* 1981
10. *Aspects of Programming for Teaching Unit Design and Development I. A practical course,* 380Z version, Wells, C, Council for Educational Technology, in preparation
11. *Taxonomy of Educational Objectives: the classification of educational goals — Handbook II: Affective domain,* Krathwohl, D R, Bloom, B S, Nasia, B B, pp176 – 185, McKay, 1964
12. *Micros in the Mathematics Classroom,* Shell/ITMA, 14 program teaching units, Longman Micro Software, 1982

SCAN 1M code sheet (see page 51)

RESOURCES (R =)	ACTIVITY LEVEL	EPISODE LEVEL (SUMMARY)
TM — teacher produced material	E — Exposition teacher to whole class (E_w) or group of 5 or more (E_n)	D — Defining
		I — Initiating activity
PMB — printed material (books)		CO — Coaching
		E — Explaining (new material)
PMC — printed material (Cards)	D — Dialogue, teacher to group < 5	C — Confirming
		R — Revising
C — computer	W_n — Pupil work, in groups of n	SS — Searching successfully
OHP		SU — Searching unsuccessfully
BB	PP — Pupil-pupil dialogue (use t to prefix teacher remark)	CN — Conversing
		F — Facilitating
		AR — Arguing (resolved)
	T — Teacher initiated	AU — Arguing (unresolved)
	P — Pupil initiated	CP — Competing
	MISCELLANEOUS	
	$\frac{t}{x}$ — teacher slip	® — resource in use
	$\frac{c}{x}$ — computer slip	®̸ — use ended
	z — major tactical change	

EVENT LEVEL

Social, organizational, procedural

g — gambit
m — managerial
ch — question for checking
v — vote
o — observation
w — withdraws statement
l — leaves discussion

Associated with content

q — question of content,
   ∧ — repeated
a — assertion
e — explanation
x — giving example
cc — conclusion
b — 'boing'
s — suggestion
i — instruction/initiation
cf — confirmation
r — rejection
k — correction

FATE OF QUESTIONS
✓— correctly answered
v — partly correct

x — answer incorrect
h́ — consistent hypothesis offered
$_h^x$ — inconsistent hypothesis offered

QUALIFIERS

Prefix p for pupil remark

Nature of activity or depth of remark

α — recall, single fact, single act, no processing involved

ß — exercise of straightforward nature, putting together several facts or acts

ɣ — extension of previous work involving new ideas

Situation or level of guidance

1 — highly structured, close direction, small number of choices

2 — some guidance offered but requires connection of facts rather than selection

3 — minimum guidance, open, investigatory

o — no pupil response
$_o^t$ — teacher does not take response
hc — hypothesis confirmed

hr — hypothesis rejected

... — time to think
( ) — off line
__ — same question